Mark C. Little

CHINA
MODERN

by Sharon Leece
photos by A. Chester Ong

PERIPLUS

Published by Periplus Editions
with editorial offices at
130 Joo Seng Road #06-01
Singapore 368357

Copyright © 2003 Periplus Editions (HK) Ltd
Text © 2003 Sharon Leece

ISBN 0 7946 0098 0
Printed in Singapore

Distributors:
North America, Latin America, and Europe
Tuttle Publishing
364 Innovation Drive
North Clarendon, VT 05759 9436, USA
Tel: (802) 773 8930; fax: (802) 773 6993
email: info@tuttlepublishing.com
www.tuttlepublishing.com

Asia Pacific
Berkeley Books Pte Ltd
130 Joo Seng Road #06-01
Singapore 368357
Tel: (65) 6280 3320; fax: (65) 6280 6290
email: inquiries@periplus.com.sg

Japan
Tuttle Publishing
Yaekari Building, 3F
5-4-12 Osaki
Shinagawa-ku
Tokyo 141 0032
Tel: (03) 5437 0171; fax: (03) 5437 0755
email: tuttle-sales@gol.com

endpaper: Handcrafted glass tiles on the bar in
TMSK restaurant, Shanghai.

page 1: Entrance to the courtyard of Ochoa-
Piccardo's villa, the Cantilever House, Beijing.

page 2: The Bamboo House's atmospheric meditation chamber-cum-tea room is surrounded by
a water-filled moat. Sliding panels of bamboo
close and open to suit the occupant's mood and
the weather conditions; views extend towards
the Great Wall, which snakes along the top of the
tree-covered slope in the distance.

this page: Architect Ed Ng created a minimal
working fireplace with uplit floating shelf in Chung
Hom Kok, Hong Kong.

Contents

The Rise of Modern China

Twenty-first century China is a country on the move. Economic reforms and modernization policies have proved catalysts for rapid change as the world's most populous country of over 1.2 billion people hurtles into the future at breakneck speed. In the aftermath of the turbulent years of the Cultural Revolution (which ended in 1976), China has been transforming itself from a nation of factory workers into one of entrepreneurs and consumers.

With its doors open and the landscape changing fast, China is undergoing a revolution of a different kind. Traditional structures and paddy fields are being replaced in the blink of an eye by futuristic neon-clad skyscrapers that are more modern metropolis than Oriental elegance. Global attention is focused on the East — Beijing will host the 2008 Olympic Games, and Shanghai the World Expo in 2010 — and a new dynamism is reaping far-reaching changes in every part of life.

What this dizzying economic and social scenario means for the design industry is an outpouring of creativity that redefines the term 'Chinese style'. Whilst in the name of progress, much of the country's architectural heritage (such as Beijing's courtyard houses and *hutongs* and Shanghai's *shikumen* houses) is, sadly, being destroyed, the calls for preservation are becoming louder and more strident. In addition, there is a fast-growing creative movement that blends the country's 5,000 years of culture with a modern outlook to produce a new vocabulary of design.

Such a rich history provides endless cultural references from which to draw inspiration. As far back as the Tang dynasty (618–907), literature, paintings, ceramics and lacquerware flourished. The Ming dynasty (1368–1644) is renowned for its elegance, balance and pared-down simplicity in terms of furniture and architecture. And the lavish opulence of the Qing dynasty (1644–1911) provided lush patterning, searing color palettes and ornate carvings.

The last time that Chinese decorative style made a major global impact was during the 17th and 18th centuries, when trading companies exported their wares to Europe. Merchants told fabulous tales of pagodas and palaces, exotic landscapes and tantalizing riches. Cargoes of silks, fragrances, spices, textiles and ceramics proved fuel for the imagination of Western craftsman who reinterpreted the designs with their visions of Oriental splendor in a decorative movement known as chinoiserie.

Now, it seems, China's time has come again. Yet today it is the classical attributes of balance, order and harmony inherent in Chinese aesthetics (especially during the Ming dynasty) that are proving the genesis for modern interpretations of the genre. Hong Kong-based architect, Ed Ng of AB Concept, believes there are three main strands of interest in classical Chinese design: "The simplicity of form. The sense of craft. And the fusion of traditional materials, such as solid wood, with modern ones, such as stainless steel and titanium."

It may seem odd, but the idea of blending Chinese accents with contemporary design ideas is a relatively new one in Hong Kong which for decades has looked to Europe for design inspiration. "Designers have now realized that good design is down to roots and foundations, rather than following whatever was popular in the West," explains Ng. Confidence is on the up: "We have learned to use our own culture as a base and absorb design philosophy and ideology from the rest of the world," says Ng.

No longer is the term "Made in China" synonymous with cheap, low-grade goods. Instead, the term now becoming associated with a new kind of chic. Shanghai-based homeware entrepreneur Choon sees a rise in quality and standards of domestic design. "No longer will China be viewed as 'copying' others. Instead a new style will evolve which will mix Chinese styles and accents with the very latest in technology and Western lifestyle."

He continues: "Because of the rather late entry of China into today's modern mainstream culture, many of today's designers are uninhibited in their styles. No one thinks twice about doing unconventional things. The boundaries of what can or cannot be done are no longer clear. This allows the unexpected to happen; which is very exciting."

Hong Kong-born and based architect Douglas Young agrees. "For me, the most exciting part of being in China as a designer is the profusion of fresh inspiration just waiting to be tapped. I believe end users in Asia are more open to new ideas. We tend to welcome change with open arms. As a designer it means experimental ideas are more easily accepted."

Nowhere is this more apparent than in China's capital Beijing. The city, well-known for its grey austerity and somber, urban developments, is also home to a thriving art and design scene which is both avant garde and experimental. Companies like property developers Redstone Industrie Ltd are bringing innovative designs to the masses with projects such as SOHO New Town (flexible modern spaces that can be used for living and working in) and the Commune at the Great Wall (eleven contemporary villas near the Great Wall of China designed by top Asian architects).

Says Redstone's Chief Architect Antonio Ochoa-Piccardo: "There is a lack of preconcepts or aesthetic rules and the freedom to assimilate all kinds of influences. China is a virgin territory to be discovered. When anything new appears it immediately goes to the wide public; nothing ever ends among a small elite. This is really exciting."

The Beijing art scene is a well of creativity, with leading artists crossing disciplines with ease. Meg Maggio, Director of the CourtYard Gallery in Beijing sees a continued growth, exploration and official recognition of artistic mediums that have spilled over into architecture, graphic design, stage design, music and other cultural fields. "This willingness to embrace individual pursuits in artistic production can be seen in all forms of cultural and artistic expression," she says.

If Beijing is China's cultural center, then Shanghai is its neon-lit, party-loving sibling, full of energy, glamor and glitz. In the 1920s and '30s, Shanghai was a cosmopolitan metropolis, which explains the legacy of different architectural styles. Grandiose art deco structures on the Bund, Tudor style mansions in the French Concession and Chinese *shikumen longtang* (stone gated alley) houses remain today and give the city a unique character. In addition to numerous gleaming high rises, new developments such as Xintiandi, a 50-hectare

(124-acre) site of boutiques, bars, restaurants and galleries modeled on 19th century *shikumen* houses, are changing the face of the city. It is places like these that draw Shanghai's increasingly hip and design-conscious population, who go to wine, dine, see, and be seen.

Such an appetite for the new is a powerful driving force behind China's rapid pace. *China Modern* explores the most exciting and dynamic contemporary interiors in Beijing, Shanghai, and Hong Kong, many never before published. The breadth of vision is astounding and each of the four chapters reveals distinctly different approaches to contemporary living in China.

'New China Chic' shows how a fresh design aesthetic — distinctly Chinese yet lively and new — has been born out of the country's rich history. Vibrant interpretations of age-old ideas include a renovated Ming dynasty courtyard house filled with contemporary art, a *shikumen* house with an interior made of hand-carved glass and a former factory turned into a hip eatery. 'Beijing Avant Garde' focuses on innovative interiors with an international edge. Highlights include a modernist villa made of bamboo, a utilitarian concrete courtyard house and a Bauhaus-inspired stone house which oozes good feng shui.

More Ming minimalist than Oriental opulent, 'The Tao of Design' explores the sense of harmony inherent in classical Chinese design, showing how natural materials, subtle colors and streamlined spaces prove the perfect antidote to the stresses of modern living. Finally, 'Echoes of the Past' reveals what happens when decorative elements from the East and West are applied to traditional structures — from Qing courtyard houses to 1930s art deco apartment blocks.

The most exciting aspect of modern Chinese design is that the movement is in its infancy. The strides made in the last ten years have been remarkable but there is no doubt that the country's rich design heritage will continue to inspire designers the world over.

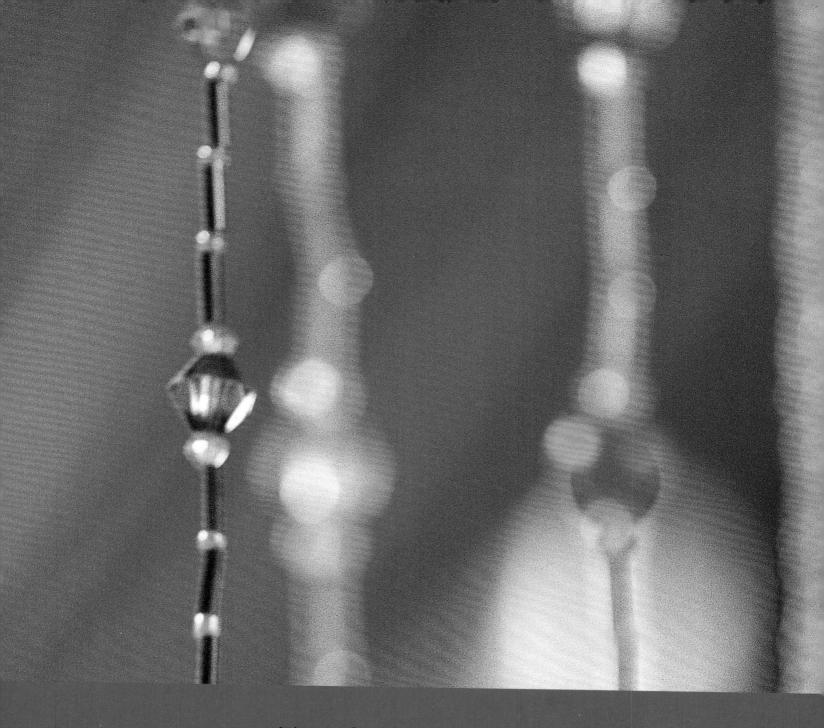

New China Chic
A new design aesthetic — distinctly Chinese yet lively and new — has been born out of China's rich history. The impact of the new Chinese style, whether at home or in the international arena, owes much to the variety of interpretations that the genre provides.

From the decorative opulence of Imperial China (cinnabar red, imperial yellow, royal purple) to the pared down classicism of the Ming dynasty (furniture and porcelain) to the rich drama of Chinoiserie (born out of the 17th and 18th century Silk Route when fabrics,

lacquerware, ceramics, and fragrances found their way to the West), China provides a vast source of inspiration.

Chinese and China-based designers are looking with a new appreciation at their heritage and are busy weaving the country's artistic and cultural traditions into their work to produce a new language of design. Particularly in cosmopolitan urban areas, centuries-old ideas are being reworked and reinterpreted — to look fresh, interesting, and totally of the moment. The new Chinese aesthetic has come of age with glamor, style, and panache.

Right: Detail of the fluorescent industrial piping offset by a baroque gilt banister.

Far right: A shocking palette of pink and gold is on the menu at The Pink Loft. At the entrance, an oversized crystal chandelier hangs low over a lily pond.

Pretty in Pink
Sizzling colors spice up a hip eatery

As night falls over Beijing, queues of taxis discharge their passengers along the tree-lined avenues and side streets of the Sanlitun embassy district. This is the city's liveliest and most compact nightlife zone, with countless bars, restaurants and cafes, ranging from the cool to the artsy to the really rather tacky. It is here that fashion-conscious Beijingers, expatriates, and overseas visitors congregate to drink, dine, dance, and people-watch into the early hours of the morning.

Recently arrived on the scene is the Pink Loft, an opulent restaurant with an extravagant palette of pink, gold, and dashes of turquoise. The cavernous space takes up three levels of an old factory building on Sanlitun South Street. A central atrium rises three floors and is inset with glass floors supported by turquoise metal frames. Thus diners who have a head for heights can eat looking down on a huge glittering chandelier suspended above a lily pond far below.

Designed and part-owned by Beijing-based artist, Lin Tianmiao, the Pink Loft is such a significant departure from her usual style — serene white-string wrapped objects and black-and-white photography — that it is hard to believe it has been designed by the same person. Yet Lin's foray into restaurant design has proved exuberant and entertaining: its use of lush silks, shiny gold drapes, and hand-beaded curtains produces a kitsch atmosphere that successfully mixes chinoiserie-style with bordello chic.

Left: Throughout the huge, three-storey interior, the interplay of lush silks, intricate beadwork, and brightly hued paintwork have helped turn a former industrial building into a vivid eatery.

Right: Glass floors allow diners to look down through a central atrium to the pond below. Vibrant pink silk cushions add modern glamor to the space.

Opposite: Artist Lin Tianmiao, designer of the space,
retained the building's original heating pipes, painting
them bright pink and adding
blue downlighting.

Clockwise from top left:
Lush colorways are carried
through to the details:
sparkling glassware; hand-
beaded glass curtains
tied with thick gold braid;
and cushions printed with
Chinese characters.

Magnificent Ming
Imperial grandeur restored

A Ming dynasty courtyard house in the center of Beijing is home to American-Chinese lawyer and art dealer Handel Lee. Built around 1610 for the nephew of a powerful and wicked eunuch called Wei Zhong Xian, the house came into Lee's possession in 1995.

Living in historical properties such as this is becoming increasingly popular, even as entire neighborhoods of courtyard houses are being demolished. However, the realities of making them habitable are not for the faint-hearted. Usually in advanced stages of disrepair, these old buildings lack even basic heating, plumbing, and electrical systems.

It was no different for Lee, who took a year and a half to renovate the tumbledown structure. He managed to retain the original front and the middle portions of the house but had to rebuild the back section as it had suffered extensive water damage. To turn what was a series of dark and drafty houses into an airy, open living space, he tore down internal walls to let in more light and installed a vaulted glass ceiling over a small courtyard between the living room building (to the fore) and the bedroom building (behind). This created a naturally-lit lounge area that links the two spaces.

The next challenge was to furnish the interior. Lee says, "I didn't want to use Chinese furniture as I find that too predictable. But the house needed its interior design to have a relationship with the past." So he used a combination of modern furniture, antique collectibles and an extensive collection of contemporary Chinese art to fill the atmospheric space. "It goes well with the house," Lee explains. "It's the contrast that makes it interesting."

Above: Accessories include antique collectibles, such as ceramic figurines and a Khymer head.

Right: Handel Lee's courtyard house, which dates back to the Ming dynasty, comprises three buildings, separated by courtyards and walkways. An informal lounge area lies between the main living room (left) and bedroom (right). This space was originally a small rear courtyard that Lee glassed in to create more living space. Latticed timber windows, which would originally have faced onto a courtyard, provide privacy without sacrificing light.

Left: The main living room features the original beams. Modern furniture and art contrast with the traditional architecture and include a hand-carved red lacquer dining table and chairs and a painting by Wang Jianwei. Hanging from the ceiling is a mobile by American artist Paul Hopkins (see right).

Below: A pair of traditional red lacquer doors marks the entrance to the house. Above the pair of chairs by Shao Fan is a painting on paper by Lu Qing.

Kaleidoscope Color
Exuberant glass art fills every inch of space

The eye-popping glass interior of TMSK restaurant in Xintiandi aims to evoke a strong sense of contemporary Chinese culture by drawing on the country's rich history. Its creators are Taiwanese glass artists Chang Yi and his wife Loretta Yang Hui-shan, former film director and movie star respectively.

TMSK is an acronym of Tou Ming Si Kao, which roughly translates as Crystal Mind. "We were bored by minimalism," explains Chang Yi. "It is too safe. We thought, as Chinese, what is the most gorgeous moment in our history? We believe it was the Tang dynasty and so we collected lots of colorful references and decided to interpret it our way."

The interplay between light and shade anchors the restaurant's design, which mixes lush colored glass with gold leaf backdrops. "We thought what a dramatic effect it would have if we put the gold leaf in the background and allowed light to flicker off it," says Chang Yi.

The project took 26 months' design work and involved an extraordinary commitment to detail. The result is that everything in the restaurant, from the interior design to the furniture and tableware, was made by Liuligongfang glass craftsmen in their own studio. There is a huge ground floor bar made of purple, blue, orange, and green glass tiles; bar stools enclosed in oval red silk lanterns; a spectacular curved gold glass ceiling inspired by the Dunhuang grottos in Gansu province; and a shimmering orchid lake underlit with neon blue light. Hand-carved pillars, intricate tiles, and lush private rooms merge gothic, baroque, and opulent into one heady mix that brings China's cultural richness to a wider audience.

Top: The double happiness symbol is carved onto fiber optic light shades.

Above: High stools with carved latticework backs are positioned in a row opposite the main bar.

Right: Vibrant colors inside; traditional 19th century *shikumen* rowhouse style in the dining area outside.

Below: The dramatic ten-meter-long (33-ft) bar on the ground floor is entirely made of glass tiles in exuberant washes of color. Gold-leaf covers the ceiling and the rear wall; gold crystal glass lights hang above.

Opposite: Downstairs, the tranquil Orchid Lake is a modern interpretation of the traditional Chinese teahouse. Atmospheric blue underlighting bouncing off the water emphasizes the Tang dynasty-inspired gold leaf walls. In front stands a pair of armchairs covered in lush, floral-print silk.

Top left: Detail of colorful hand-carved tiles inset into the bar. According to ancient beliefs, the circle is a symbol of heaven; the square a symbol of earth.

Bottom left: The red silk bar stools are in the shape of an inverted 1930s Shanghai lantern.

Left: View along the length of the Orchid Lake where each orchid is made of hand-carved glass. At the end, a mirrored wall works to reflect the dramatic space with its blue and violet lighting. Lighting is key throughout the restaurant: with the focus on the interplay of light and shade to create washes of color and shadowy corners. To the left, cosy seating areas are divided by wooden pillars and beams.

Below: Glass artists Chang Yi and his wife Loretta Yang Huishan used hand-carved glass to create TMSK, including walls, screens, floors, windows, tables, chairs, and table-ware. Upstairs, a wall of ornate carved glass pillars topped with jade green spheres marks the entrance to a private dining room.

Right: The central feature of the first floor dining room is a domed glass ceiling inspired by the 1,600-year-old Dunhuang grottos in Gansu province, the world's greatest repository of Buddhist art. The ceiling subtly changes color, moving from gold to red to green to pink.

Temple of Heaven
An exchange of cultures

Above: Sculptural glass vases by French design duo Tsé & Tsé are juxtaposed against old wooden window frames. Outside hangs a traditional silk lantern.

Right: Chinese doorways appear in a variety of shapes. As dusk falls, this dramatic red moongate frames the secluded court-yard. The color red signifies joy and good fortune.

A restored courtyard house located in the grounds of a temple north of Beijing's Forbidden City is now the distinctive home of French architect Pascale Desvaux and her family. In keeping with traditional Chinese architectural emphasis on enclosure and separation, the house is encircled by a wall that protects the interior from the world outside. "The idea was to take elements of Chinese architecture and history and to incorporate them with contemporary style," explains the architect, who completely renovated the 350-square-meter (3,766-sq-ft) space before moving in.

An impressive terracotta red archway featuring a moongate leads into a courtyard garden. Desvaux uses the moongate as her primary linkage motif within the interior, where modern moongates, painted midnight blue, are installed in the middle of each interior wall to produce a long slim space that flows around the courtyard on three sides. This linking device adds to the balance and symmetry of the interior and is a practical as well as an aesthetic decision. "The rooms are not very big so this saves a lot of space," she explains.

Hers is a clever fusion of styles that values the power of simplicity. The palette is bold: the intense blue of the moongates contrasts with the traditional green, yellow, and red color scheme of Chinese temples, retained in the painted pillars, beams, and intricately patterned exterior woodwork. Inside, it is a stylish and comfortable home filled with Cassina sofas, antique Chinese furniture, own-design pieces, and curios from Beijing's Panjiayuan flea market. It is a little slice of heaven in the heart of the city.

Below: A series of modern, midnight blue moongates link the rooms inside the courtyard house. This is the view from the bedroom of the long, slim living room, which is furnished with a combination of antique furniture found in Beijing and Desvaux's own designs.

Right: By applying a contemporary design ethos to a traditional structure, Pascsale Desvaux aims to create an exchange between cultures. In the master bedroom, the red silk painting is by Zhao Ling and the Vietnamese bedlinen is by Catherine Denoual. The Constanza floor lamp is by Luceplan.

Clockwise from top left: Flea market finds include shagreen spectacles cases, circular yellow roof tiles with dragon motifs and calligraphy print cushions. Below, painted pillars and woodwork retain the traditional red and green palette. The overhanging roof with upturned eaves protects the house from the elements whilst letting sunlight through.

Opposite: The moongate is a traditional Chinese symbol of happiness. When closed, it provides privacy inside the courtyard.

X Appeal
Fashion-forward designs, proudly made in China

Australian designer Anthony Xavier Edwards has been living in Shanghai for eight years. He moved to the city after spending time in Japan and other Asian countries, and, inspired by the city's textile culture, he began producing statement-making silk scarves. Today, he displays his own form of Shanghai glamor in his Xintiandi boutique, called X, where alongside fabulously flamboyant fashions (silks, organzas, hand dyed ostrich feathers), he offers hats, soft furnishings, ceramics, and acid-etched glassware, all bearing the label "Proudly Made in China."

Such chic, domestic designs are proof that China-made goods can now hold their own with panache. "There is a huge growing middle class in China that demands refinement," Edwards explains. He finds his adopted country a limitless source of inspiration: "There's something in the environment that gives you a buzz. I'm inspired by so many things China has given me." He sums up his look as stylish classics with a flamboyant edge — "I want to do bits of madness that make a woman smile" — and it is an approach that translates into his home environment.

Edwards lives in a modern apartment block in the French Concession, a short taxi ride from Xintiandi and has furnished it with his own-design pieces that are a Chinese-Western fusion. "It's my own version of chinoiserie," he says. His is a theatrical, exuberant environment: lots of black and gold, ostrich feather-trimmed Chinese silk cushions, slim CD cabinets modeled on pagodas, a black lacquer bamboo motif screen, and art deco style armchairs. "And all of it has been made in China over the last eight years."

Top: Side lamp using a traditional painted Mandarin (official) figure as a base.

Above: Acid-etched glass pots with motifs inspired by the ballroom of Shanghai's Peace Hotel and by a fragment of China's oldest carpet, made 5,500 years ago.

Right: The chinoiserie-style living room contains Edward's own-design furniture, including a curvaceous art deco inspired armchair and a lacquered side cabinet with delicate floral motif.

Left: The home studio is filled with fabrics, beads and accessories. Two mannequins are draped with examples of Edward's flamboyant Chinese-inspired fashions, which have proved popular with the city's glamor set.

Below: A tasseled box rests on a chinoiserie-style silk scarf.

Bottom: A silver bust of Mao Zedong.

Right: "Nothing should be ordinary," maintains the designer. In a baroque corner of the living room is a black lacquer screen with bamboo motifs and a black and gold silk upholstered art deco armchair accessorized with animal print cushions and an ostrich feather throw.

Below: The bedroom features a striking geometric palette of black, white, and red softened by a white lace bedspread.

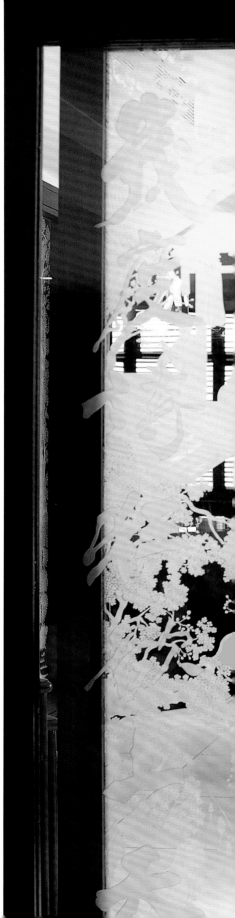

Far Pavilion
Minimalist Ming-style proportions

When Loretta and Lawrence Lee moved into their apartment on Hong Kong island's leafy Tai Hang Road, they wanted to create a tranquil, streamlined home with Oriental influences, both old and new. "I wanted clean lines and a neutral palette," says Loretta. "I also liked the subtle, simple look of Ming-style Chinese furniture."

The decorative foundations of their 279-square-meter (3,000-sq-ft) home were based around a 20-year-old set of classic etched-glass panels inherited from Lawrence's father. Architectural designer Simon Lee of Persimmon Home devised an octagonal 'Pavilion Room' with a stepped-up ceiling based on classical Chinese architecture and positioned it at the rear of the living room. He then clad the panels with a cherrywood veneer frame to make a transparent corridor-facing wall and a pair of sliding entry doors to enclose the space.

Simplicity of form and tactile materials, including *wenge*-stained *huali* wood furniture and cool white marble, produce a classic yet harmonious interior devoid of superfluous detail. European designer pieces, such as a chandelier by Gino Sarfatti and bathroom fittings by Philippe Starck, fuse with custom-made Persimmon Home Chinese furniture created with modern living in mind: a Chinese wedding cabinet with sliding doors and a set of four low horseshoe-back armchairs designed to slip under a mahjong table.

"Ming style furnishings have great potential to work with clean-cut modern spaces because they complement each other so well," explains Simon Lee. "Their Zen-like calmness appeals to many people who live a metropolitan life and who want a calm, mellow home to retreat to."

Above: Delicate white china dinnerware looks simple and elegant when pared with silver-grey placemats.

Right: Panels of 20-year-old etched glass featuring Chinese characters and pastoral scenes have been clad in cherrywood veneer frames to form the sliding doors to an octagonal pavilion room. Low-back armchairs (based on the traditional horseshoe-back armchair) by Persimmon Home have been scaled down to fit under a custom-made mahjong table. All are made of *huali* wood with a *wenge* stain. Behind hangs a pair of 50-year-old silk embroidered calligraphy couplets.

Clockwise from left: A pair of Ming-style official's hat armchairs flank a *huali* wood sideboard, which features two 1930s style table lamps. Above the lamps, a Lee family etched glass panel is set into a custom-made steel frame.

Detail of spider orchids.

One side of the master bedroom is converted into a dressing room complete with a large mirror and fitted cabinets clad in cherrywood veneer. The floor is made of *zitan* wood.

A cluster of candles and essential oil burners in the living room.

Opposite: The guest bathroom features copper mosaic tiles hung vertically instead of horizontally. A large cherrywood framed mirror covers the rear wall. The wash-basin unit is based on traditional Ming-style proportions.

Tee Time
Classical architecture refined and updated

Right: The 2,000-square-meter (21,528-sq-ft) residential villas of the Fuchun Resort have been built in the style of the Southern Song dynasty (AD 1127–1279) with the emphasis on simplicity and graceful lines. A series of spaces works to lead the eye inwards, with one vista opening up to reveal another.

Above: Detail oriented — each alcove features a fresh orange in an iron housing.

The Fuchun Resort is a three hours' drive along the recently-built Hangzhou-bound expressway from Shanghai. Set against a backdrop of the rolling Fuyang hills, the resort comprises a series of secluded villas and a Zen-like golf clubhouse that stand amid a scenic terraced landscape planted with row upon row of green tea bushes.

This part of China, known as Jiangnan, or "south of the Yangtze river", is noted for its scenery, history, culture, art, and production of green tea. The story goes that in AD 1347, when one of the four masters of Yuan dynasty painting, Huang Gongwang, retired to his hometown of Fuyang in the Fuchun mountains, he created a pen and ink scroll of this pastoral paradise and aptly called it "Living in the Fuchun Mountains". This painting is today considered a national treasure.

It is this history of culture and art that provided the inspiration for the resort's design, which blends traditional elements with modern comforts. The freestanding, courtyard style villas look to typical Jiangnan architectural elements, such as white walls and neat elegant lines, in a bid to fit into the terrain. They nestle in small, private groups in the village tradition, scattered around the complex.

The ambience is subtle, relaxed, and modern, with a harmony that is Chinese in essence. Soaring vaulted wooden beamed ceilings and structural pillars produce cavernous yet luxurious spaces with echoes of a classical past. Materials, too, are natural and understated: inkstone, wood, stone, slate, wicker, and iron coupled with leather, bamboo, rattan, and silk. Each villa offers expansive views over the surrounding hills, a series of endless pastoral vistas.

Opposite: In the Fuchun Resort's clubhouse, an oversized urn provides a dramatic centerpiece to a courtyard lake. Bamboo blinds shield the interior spaces from the sunlight.

Right: The clubhouse corridors are furnished with clean-lined antique wood furniture and vibrant contemporary art. This Rose Chair, with its low back and armrests, would traditionally have been placed under a window in a traditional Chinese house as it would not block the view.

Above: Stone pillars and exposed timber beams create an impressive framework in the cavernous spa where the emphasis is on health, relaxation and rejuvenation. The proportions of the space are symmetrical and include two negative-edge spa pools: one hot and one cold.

Right: A shelving unit filled with towels and red lacquer boxes is modeled on pared-down Ming dynasty lines.

Above: Perfect proportions — the clubhouse changing rooms reflect the commitment to balance in the traditional Chinese aesthetic. A tall ceramic urn is positioned above an antique recessed leg bench.

Left: Unfurling vistas — corridors lead to interior courtyards, which reduce the inside-outside divide.

Opposite: In the clubhouse restaurant, lines are kept simple and natural materials work to create an elegant, understated palette.

Clockwise from right: The Noodle Bar is made of matt inkstone. Diners perch on a traditional bench whilst eating. Signature tableware includes river stones and condiment dishes used as chopsticks rests.

Pure Glamor
A new jazz age on The Bund

Above: The Bund's neo-classical edifices light up at night to reveal an impressive panorama of Shanghai's architectural history.

Left: Sleek and sophisticated, the Glamor Room bar and restaurant offers a hip reworking of the city's seedy yet romantic past. Styled around a 1930s Hollywood movie set, its sunken lounge area exhibits dark parquet flooring, lush claret upholstery, and impressive views over the Bund.

Nothing sums up the glamor of old Shanghai like the Bund, once the city's chief shipping, trading, and financial district. Things may have changed, but the grandiose Western architectural façades dating back to the early 20th century still line the Huangpu River to the West.

While to the East the new Shanghai rises in the form of Pudong district's futuristic skyscrapers, the Bund is undergoing a transformation of its own. Entrepreneurs are seeing the value in its grand old structures and are putting them to other uses. One of the first to do so was restaurateur Michelle Garnaut, who opened M on the Bund in 1999. She chose Number 5 The Bund, originally the Nisshin Kisen Kaisha Building, erected in 1925 for the Japanese shipping line that plied the Chinese coast and the Yangtze.

The restaurant quickly became the most fashionable dining spot in town. It was followed in 2001 by the high-gloss Glamor Room and Bar on the same floor and with views over the back of The Bund. Designed by Roger Hackworth and Debra Little, the Glamor Room is based on a 21st century impression of a 1930s Hollywood movie set, with silver plated fluted columns, sparkling curtains of crystal beads, and art deco-inspired touches of copper, bronze, and nickel. Woven grass wall coverings, smoky plum velour upholstery, dark parquet flooring, and antique Chinese tables add a sexy, sensuous air. "The Glamor Room happened organically and I felt Shanghai was ready for it," says Garnaut. "It looks so glamorous and sophisticated and reminiscent of Shanghai's seedy past; I feel it is aptly named."

Above: Curtains of sparking crystal beads and woven grass wall coverings add a modern edge to the art deco inspirations. "Shanghai is ready for a bar for grown-ups," says owner Michelle Garnaut, "and that is exactly what the sexy, sophisticated atmosphere here has created."

Clockwise from top left:
A huge crystal curtain can be pulled across to seal off a second wine and dine area.

Patterned velour stools based on art deco designs provide relaxed seating in the bar area.

Reflective surfaces abound, including a set of three signature silver-plated fluted columns. Antique wooden Chinese furniture provides a warm contrast to the cool metals.

Lamps feature bases made from glass beads found in Shanghai flea markets.

Beijing Avant Garde

As China races into the future, the capital city of Beijing is fast becoming a hotbed of creativity. In everything from architecture to art, fashion to film, a revolution in style is producing a modern aesthetic that is both and creative.

More Ming minimalist than Oriental opulent, designers are proving that "Made in China" is no longer synonymous with cheap, mass production. Simplicity and experimentalism are the order of the day, especially in the fields of architecture and design, where quality work is defined by balance, clarity, and restraint.

Nowhere is this more apparent than in the fields of architecture and design. And whilst innovative residential structures — from Bauhaus-inspired homes in the countryside to modernist villas by the Great Wall of China — may be based on the most international of ideas, the roots have not been forgotten. The age-old Chinese desire to commune with the natural environment — whether in terms of bringing the outdoors inside, creating harmony with nature, or in the local materials used for construction — remains a major source of inspiration, no matter how revolutionary the design.

The Furniture House
An experimental house made of bamboo

Above: An airy terrace open to the elements leads off from the main reception area. It is furnished with a simple daybed with a woven rattan seat. Traditionally daybeds had various uses: as a sitting platform during the day and as a bed at night.

Right: Shigeru Ban's court-yard house works to dissolve the boundaries between inside and out. The materials used — bamboo, glass, white marble — look elegantly understated when viewed from the entranceway looking into the minimal square courtyard.

The Commune by the Great Wall is a development of 11 modern villas, designed by top Asian architects, located next to the Great Wall of China near Beijing. Among these is The Furniture House, by Japanese architect Shigeru Ban, a serene, one-storey villa that comprises a main central courtyard and rooms arranged around it in a simple square format.

Ban has a reputation for using technology and materials in innovative ways. For The Furniture House, he devised a bamboo veneer lumber to create prefabricated furniture to be used as the main structural component as well as the exterior and interior walls. "This is the first time bamboo has been used as a structural element," says Antonio Ochoa-Piccardo, Chief Architect at the site.

During his research, Ban discovered that bamboo plywood, with its woven patterns on the outer layer, felt as strong as the structural veneer plywood used in Japan. He explained, "I thought, if it was possible to laminate strips of bamboo into plywood, then it would of course be possible to construct LVL (laminated veneer lumber) out of bamboo. Moreover, all exterior and interior finishes on the walls as well as the flooring could be done in bamboo to ensure consistency of materials throughout the project."

The extensive use of bamboo, coupled with the villa's glass-walled central courtyard and white marble floors, yields an elegant spatial organization that is both technologically innovative and aesthetically pleasing. It is a design with an aura of quiet confidence.

Above: A row of bamboo veneer cabinets lines the living room. Such built-in furniture appears throughout the house, working not just to define the spaces but as vital structural elements. Floor-to-ceiling glass walls allow exterior views to be a key element in the space.

Left: Curvaceous white leather chairs by Idée are arranged around the dining table. A wall of built-in cubilinear bamboo shelves is filled with earthenware and glass accessories.

Below: Lack of color has a calming effect. In the dining room, bamboo trees cast their shadows through the Roman blinds.

The Bamboo Wall
Beautiful bamboo: inside and out

Japanese architect Kenjo Kuma is the man behind the most talked-about villa at the Commune by the Great Wall. Kuma was inspired by the Great Wall itself and his bamboo- and glass-fronted house — The Bamboo Wall — was created in the same way that the Great Wall runs over the Shuiguan mountains: "The formal quality of the wall running along the undulating ridgeline without being isolated from the environment was the nature we were attracted to. Our intention was to apply this nature of The Great Wall to the act of dwelling."

Bamboo was chosen because "it is a material that is indigenous to Japan and to China, so is a symbol of the meeting of the two". Bamboo is also light, strong, flexible, and sustainable, symbolizes longevity and, according to the tenets of feng shui, brings luck and prosperity to the home.

This versatile material lines the walls, divides the rooms, and even forms some of the floors. From some points inside the villa it seems as if you are looking through layer upon layer of bamboo forest of different densities and diameters. Bamboo also creates the centerpiece of Kuma's design: a serene meditation chamber-cum-tea room complete with sliding panels and a water-filled moat that looks out over a forested hillside to the Great Wall high above.

It is a minimal environment that allows an easy interplay between interior and exterior, allowing nature to be the key element, both inside and out.

Above: Kenjo Kuma's Bamboo Wall house is part of the Commune by the Great Wall project. The award-winning development was originated by property developers Zhang Xin and Pan Shiyi of Beijing-based SOHO China Ltd. The brief was direct and to the point: use local materials and retain the original topography of the area. Today the villas function as a boutique hotel.

Right: The house lies in a valley near the Shuiguan section of The Great Wall of China. Kuma uses nature as a key design element with floor-to-ceiling glass walls, some lined with bamboo poles, to reduce the inside-outside divide. Woven rattan furniture and neutral upholstery further emphasize the natural theme.

Above: Bamboo is used decoratively as well as structurally. Here, it looks fresh and of-the-moment when juxtaposed against a contemporary, grey felt modular sofa.

Left: Looking from the dining room into the raised kitchen area. Bamboo is frequently used to divide the villa into different areas whilst retaining an open plan atmosphere. The black slate floors increase the Zen-like feel of the space.

Above: Tatami mats have been used extensively in the almost monastic bedrooms. Peach silk bedlinens add muted warmth to the restful spaces.

The Cantilever House
Soaring over the valley floor

Antonio Ochoa-Piccardo's eye-catching Cantilever House, with its sienna-washed concrete and southern elmwood exterior, appears to hang suspended over a slope, with the front soaring out over the valley floor and the back nestling cosily into the hillside.

Ochoa-Piccardo, Redstone Industrie's chief architect and a long-time China resident (he is originally from Venezuela) based his villa on its relationship with the surrounding landscape. "You can feel the mountain entering the house and in the front you can also see a view of the mountain." His distinctive color choice was also based on the natural environment. "Originally the house was in concrete but I felt that grey would be too much of a contrast. So we stained it with a sienna pigment which allows it to be somehow part of the landscape," he explains.

Accessed by a sweeping cut grey slate entrance stairway, visitors wind their way inside to find a sensuous series of open spaces that flow seamlessly into one another. From the spacious, light-filled double-height living area to external and internal terraces to the bedrooms arranged in a square around the edges of the cube, the spaces are all integrated. The Cantilever House also features a rooftop garden, Jacuzzi, and barbecue unit. "One of the lessons we learnt from modern architect Le Corbusier was that the land your house takes should be replaced. Here I am doing that with a rooftop garden," says Ochoa. One can walk up a ramp stretching from the back of the house and turning back on itself to end on the roof. The effect is akin to heading into the hills for a private picnic.

Top: Ochoa-Piccardo's villa is designed to jut out into the valley to the fore and nestle into the hillside to the rear, thus becoming part of the landscape.

Above: The geometrical cube motif is integral to the interior and exterior architecture.

Opposite: The light-filled villa has been designed so that the interior spaces flow seamlessly into one another. The double-height living room looks onto a grass-clad slope at the rear, which provides access to the rooftop garden.

Left: Light streams into the entrance to the courtyard, falling in pools on the grey slate wall. The warm, natural colors, and textures emphasize the villa's harmonious relationship with the landscape.

Opposite: Ochoa-Piccardo designed his villa as a series of integrated spaces, all of which can be enjoyed separately but are connected visually. Here the courtyard acts as a semi-enclosed space, easing the transition between inside and out.

Modern Romance
A secluded fortress in the countryside

The foothills of Changping county, to the north of Beijing, provide the picturesque setting for lawyer and art collector Handel Lee's minimalist country retreat. Accessed by car along a winding, unpaved road, the first glimpse of the white concrete structure is from across a lake as it sits quietly against the hillside.

Lee collaborated with photographer-turned-architect Gao Bo to create this romantic ideal. "The house had to be simple, almost pure, something that could be juxtaposed against the natural landscape. So we did a hard modern structure that kind of floats there."

The contrast continues on reaching the house. Visitors enter through a fortress-like courtyard, an empty square space with soaring nine-meter-high (29.5 ft) walls. Lee explains: "On the way to the house you are surrounded by nature, water, greenery, and birds. Then you hit this courtyard structure — it's very clean. The height was built purposefully to block out everything so you see nothing except for sky and walls. It's very dramatic."

The one-storey 380-square-meter (4090-sq-ft) interior is minimalist, a series of free-flowing spaces in a predominantly black-and-white palette filled with early to mid-20th century European designer classics, such as by Le Corbusier, Harry Bertoia, and Mies van der Rohe.

This house is modern by design, yet comfortable in its rural location. A rectangular cantilevered structure with floor-to-ceiling glass walls on three sides juts out towards the forest at the rear, making it hard to distinguish inside from out. As the evening mist descends, the silence is enveloping; and the house takes on a serene, calm aura, at one with the landscape outside.

Above: **A collection of ornamental stainless steel rocks by artist Zhan Wang. Traditionally, rocks were bought inside the Chinese house to satisfy a desire to return to nature.**

Right: **Handel Lee's Bauhaus-inspired house sits well in a rural environment, with its cubist lines, flat roof, and smooth façade. "When I first saw this plot of land it looked like a scene from a traditional Chinese landscape painting with its mountains, pine trees, and greenery. All that was missing was a house."**

Right: A glass-walled cantilevered room juts out into the greenery. The structure highlights the juxtaposition between the natural and non-natural environments and creates a bridge between the two.

Above: Nights can be chilly in the countryside, so an open fire and a zebra skin rug in the master bedroom add a touch of warmth to the interior.

Right: An avid contemporary Chinese art collector, Lee has created a gallery exhibition space here. Again, the pared-down environment lets attention focus on the works.

Opposite: White walls, a concrete ceiling, and black cement floors provide a hard-edged modernism to the open plan dining room. The black-and-white palette provides dramatic impact to the space.

Above: Starck minimalism in the entrance hall. The use of Bauhaus (1920s to 1940s) principles of classical architecture and pure form reflect the deep-rooted modernity inherent in Chinese design. From Taoist (600 BC) simplicity to Ming dynasty (1368–1644) elegance, such centuries-old ideas of balance and restraint prove equally applicable today.

At Home and At Work
Flexible living in a modern high rise

For Venezuelan architect Antonio Ochoa-Piccardo, the divisions between home and work are very fine indeed. A long term Beijing-resident and Chief Architect for property company Redstone Industrie, Ochoa-Piccardo lives with his wife and children in what is touted to be one of the city's hippest neighborhoods.

SOHO New Town is a Redstone Industrie success story and consists of numerous blocks of highrise towers livened up by blue, orange, yellow, and red trim rather than the austere grey for which Beijing is renowned. But what makes the development the residence of choice for Beijing's upper middle classes is that it offers flexible, urban units that can be used for living or working or both.

SOHO here actually stands for "Small Office, Home Office", and for Beijingers it has been a revelation. Each block comprises flexible, modern spaces built around a high-rise courtyard, divided up every four floors for residents to use. Contemporary avant garde sculptures by some of China's leading artists such as Ai Wei Wei, Li Hui, Xu Tan, and Ding Yi dot the public areas, complementing the architecture of the space.

Ochoa-Piccardo, who was responsible for designing the interiors of the units, transformed his own space into a comfortable, vibrant family home. He knocked two apartments into one and employed a colorful palette of mustard yellow, fresh blue, and deep turquoise green to offset his collections of warm wood Chinese furniture and contemporary furnishings. Banks of windows running the length of the apartment afford panoramic views across the city.

Top: "Tilted House", a concrete and steel sculpture by artist Ai Wei Wei stands in one of the residential towers in Beijing's SOHO New Town.

Above: In the entrance foyer of Redstone Industrie Co's Beijing offices is a fiberglass sculpture, "Dreaming Pig" by Xu Tan.

Opposite: Rich mustard walls, cream upholstery, and warm wood Chinese furniture define Ochoa-Piccardo's living room.

Left: Multi-use — a compact guest room-cum-lounging area is positioned at the end of the living room. Sliding doors on each side can be closed for privacy or opened out to make the room part of the general living space. The raised bed base conceals a mattress, which can be slid out and put on top of the tatami mats when needed.

Below: A red and black leather footstool makes a striking contrast to the wooden altar table, found in a Beijing market.

Clockwise from top left:
In the entrance hall is a pair of mid-20th century folding chairs that would once have been used in a traditional tea house, pulled out to seat audiences gathering for short operas and other presentations. The black-and-white photographs behind are by Venezuelan photographer Jose Sigala.

Strong colors — yellow, green, and blue — are used as striking backdrops to traditional chairs sourced in Beijing. "Our criteria for buying old furniture is the design and the use of good materials. When you look at these chairs you can see they have been used a lot," says the architect.

Art World
Contemporary Chinese art in a modernist structure

In 1999, art collector Frank Uytterhaegen founded the China Art Archives and Warehouse with artist Ai Wei Wei and the late Chinese art scholar Hans van Dijk. The following year they built a house and gallery in Cao Chang Di district to offer contemporary artists a professional space to present their works. "Our initial idea was to create something very minimalist using materials from Beijing," explains Uytterhaegen. "It had to have lots of light inside, space to show artworks and gardens which were private and cosy."

Today, high brick walls surround the complex, which comprises a gallery and a two-storey house arranged around a central grass-lawned courtyard. Both interiors showcase a wide collection of modern Chinese art, much of it experimental. Uytterhaegen explains, "We are interested in all aspects of the contemporary art scene and prefer quality and innovativeness compared to the purely commercial approach."

His home is a gallery in itself: spacious, modern, and minimal, with rooms that flow into one another due to the use of wall partitions instead of doors. Industrial styling includes concrete floors, slate grey or white walls, and an open-sided concrete stairwell that links the two levels. Furnishings are few but carefully chosen, ranging from valuable antiques to everyday objects, including Tibetan cupboards, Neolithic pottery, Ming furniture, and local farmers' chairs. Paintings by artists Ding Yi, Li Dafang, and Qi Zhilong line the walls: all are part of a 300-piece private collection owned by Uytterhaegen's Modern Chinese Art Foundation, which works to bring contemporary Chinese art to a broader audience.

Top: At the top of the stairs stands a large Han dynasty (206 BC–AD 220) ceramic horse; to the right is the painting "Horse Head" by Yin Zhaoyang. On top of the Ming dynasty (1368–1644) table is a piece of Yang Shao pottery.

Right: Ceramic collections are arranged along the study table.

Opposite: Frank Uytterhaegen's house has been designed to show off the collections of contemporary Chinese art to best effect. Interior colors and textures have been kept low-key and the free-flowing spaces provide a calming backdrop to the artworks. In the entrance hall hangs "Self Portrait" by Li Dafang.

Above: In the home office, a dividing wall has been partially cut away to allow glimpses into the living room, giving an open feel but retaining spatial separation. To the left hangs a painting "Beyond Youth" by Yin Zhaoyang; other artworks include 19th century portraits and Cultural Revolution style paintings.

Above: On the living room side of the wall — a pair of Ming-style sloping stile cabinets topped with a collection of Neolithic pottery. More pottery adorns a Ming dynasty stand; to the left is a painted Tibetan cabinet.

Right: In the entrance hall, a pair of paintings entitled "Mao Girls" by Qi Zhilong hangs on a whitewashed exposed brick wall.

Left: An old door has been made into a country-style table and is flanked by traditional farmers' stools in the dining room. Pine wood storage cabinets run the length of the right-hand side of the room. The walls and ceiling are finished with waxed plaster, the floor is concrete.

Below: Above the stone sink, "Computer Controlled by Pig Brain" by Guangdong-born artist Zheng Guogu hangs on the wall.

Above: Less is more in this architecturally minimal interior. Here the eye is drawn to "Appearance of Crosses", 1995, by Ding Yi, which hangs on a bare white wall. The pared-down space is punctuated by collections of antique Chinese furniture and carpets.

Concrete Abode
An artistically austere home
and studio

Avant garde artist Ai Wei Wei's studio-cum-home in Beijing's Chao Chang Di district is an exercise in tactile utilitarianism. "The scale, proportion, and proper use of basic materials are the most important elements of architecture," explains the Beijing-born artist, who favored local materials in the construction of his residence.

Reflecting the fast pace of life in modern China, Ai Wei Wei designed and executed his home in only seven months, including a construction time of just 100 days. The complex is surrounded by high walls: inside a stylishly austere grey brick structure rises around a modern grass-lawned courtyard. The building has a reinforced concrete skeleton-frame structure, which is left exposed internally. On the inside, walls and beams are either left raw or feature white slab brickwork, reddish brick panels, or a grey-blue wax plaster finish.

The free-flowing 500-square-meter (1,640-sq-ft) space within is loft-like, with raw finishes adding warmth to a minimal interior. The entrance door leads into the cavernous, two-storey-high living space with its one huge window providing the light. An open, raw concrete stairway leads up to bedrooms and a workspace. Furniture is primarily antique Chinese, which adds to the subdued neutral tones.

This is also a place of work, and Ai Wei Wei's expansive studio, also two storeys high, is set at right angles to the main living space. Once again the echoing space is windowless, but light pours in through two huge skylights. Here, as in the main living area, the atmosphere is serene and contemplative, devoid of any superfluous excesses.

Above: Independent artist Ai Wei Wei's Beijing home is almost fortress-like with its grey brickwork, interior grassed courtyard and high surrounding walls.

Right: Raw finishes — to the right of the two-storey high living room, furnished sparely with select pieces of unlacquered Chinese furniture, is a pair of opaque glass doors that lead into the artist's studio. An open concrete stairwell accesses the upper level of bedrooms and study.

Left: Concrete, red brick, and wood — the materials used in the construction of the house and for the interior furnishings were kept to a minimum to create a soothing yet tactile palette.

Below: On the upper level, piles of art books balance on a country-style table. Inset into the wax plaster wall is a window looking down into the studio below.

Opposite: The meticulous architectural proportions of the living room are revealed by the view from the kitchen area at the rear. A floor-to-ceiling wood-framed window is the sole natural light source. Furniture is kept to a minimum; each wooden piece carefully positioned to maximize the dramatic impact of the space. The centerpiece is a large pine work-cum-dining table surrounded by antique official's hat armchairs, which have been stripped of lacquer.

Left: In the artist's studio, a pair of skylights high above provides lots of natural light. The cavernous space offers ample room for creation and display. Against the walls balance Ai Wei Wei's quirky Chinese tables, reconfigured into sculptures. On the worktable is a 33-meter-long (108 ft) acrylic on silk work by artist Lu Qing.

Above: Open to view — in a corner on the upper level is a freestanding toilet.

Right: Ironware on the rustic wood entrance door.

Below: Detail of linen covered books.

Stone Age
Limestones, cobblestones and river stones

For Gao Bo, home is a serene Bauhaus-inspired stone house surrounded by 24 century-old persimmon trees in a quiet village in Changping county to the north of Beijing. The Harbin-born photographer, known for his haunting black-and-white portraits taken in China's most remote regions, designed and built the house himself, preferring the tranquility and space of the countryside to the convenience of inner city Beijing. The feng shui is good here too. "Placement in the north while facing the south is the most stable and secure position," Bo says. "Plus, the mountain behind this building is like the back of a chair on which people can lean on securely."

The house, which has been built from local stone materials, is divided into main two areas: a living space and a huge photographic studio. "I wished to infuse new elements into these materials by presenting them in a new form," explains Bo, who drew inspiration from the natural curves of the land and from Chinese characters and calligraphy. "Chinese calligraphy allows plenty of spontaneity in writing. This helps me a lot when I draft the floor plans, for example; I am bold enough to borrow non-architectural language to finish my design."

Huge glass windows along one side allow light to flood into the double-height space, which features a cosy bedroom on a mezzanine above. It is a comfortable space which, he admits, is filled with "a collection of memories", including his own design furniture, Chinese antiques, regional artifacts, and, of course, his portraiture. "Building a home is not the most difficult task; building a home which is in keeping with the owner's character and appearance is the real challenge."

Opposite: Photographer Gao Bo chose to build his house in a village in Changping county. "This village was the emperor's fruit farm in the Qing Dynasty, that's why it's called Shang Yuan, the Upper Court." In the masculine living room, Gao Bo's photography is juxtaposed against black leather armchairs and a ponyskin Le Corbusier chaise longue. A large glass window emphasizes the cobblestoned courtyard walls outside.

Clockwise from top left: Twenty-four persimmon trees, over 100 years old, grow in the grounds.

A water feature erupts from the floor near the main entrance to the house.

In the hallway, the image used to promote Gao Bo's photographic exhibition "Tibet, 1993–1995" stands atop a Shanxi table.

Gao Bo chose to use local materials used for generations in the construction of his home: these include limestone, cobblestones, and river stones.

Above: A wonky wooden bookcase inset into the wall of the photographic studio adds a dash of humour to this much-used workspace, filled with canvases, textbooks, and visual paraphernalia.

Above: Examples of Gao Bo's large black-and-white portraiture are propped in the corner of the studio. Huge windows run along one side to let in lots of light. The furniture is a combination of own design pieces and country-style Chinese antiques.

Above: The dining room
is a mix of Chinese and
Western influences. The
contemporary Chinese
style dining table and chairs are
of Gao Bo's own design,
constructed of iron, steel,
and wood. The pinewood
open stairs lead to a bedroom on the mezzanine
level; beneath stands an
antique rosewood cabinet.

The Tao of Design

Natural textures, streamlined interiors, and attention to the art of detailing may seem like a modern invention, but such philosophies of restraint and harmony go back centuries in Chinese culture. Today, the idea of living in an ordered, harmonious space that offers peace and relaxation, in a bid to offset the pace of modern life, has never been more appealing.

It was in around 600 BC that Chinese scholar Lao-Tzu advocated the philosophy-cum-religion of Taoism (in Chinese the word "tao" means "way"), which stressed the importance of

simplicity as the key to truth and freedom. Slightly later, Confucianism taught that propriety and ritual are key to social order.

Centuries on, the sophisticated simplicity and elegance of the Ming dynasty (1368–1644), both in terms of culture and design, is proving itself immensely desirable. These ideas have been incorporated in modern interiors and transformed into minimally designed spaces upon which elements of Chinese style have been overlain. Clever spatial discipline is the key to success, as the interiors featured in this chapter demonstrate.

Right: A pair of lion door knockers adorn the door to artist Lin Tianmiao's home.

Far right: In the large all-white studio, builders used a traditional Chinese timber framework to support the roof. It comprises thick vertical timber pillars, short vertical supports called purlins, and horizontal beams. Hence the gravitational forces are distributed downwards and then out through the wooden frame.

Artist's Retreat
An all-white studio fit for experimentation

Lin Tianmiao is considered one of China's most progressive contemporary female artists. She is best known for cocooning everyday objects, from picture frames to woks to sewing machines to bicycles, in layer upon layer of white thread. Lin resided in New York with her video artist husband Wang Gongxin for ten years but moved back to Beijing in 1995; today they live in Tong Xian, a peaceful suburb 40 kilometers (25 miles) from the city and an area favored by many members of the artistic community.

Her spacious home functions as both studio, display space, and living quarters. A pair of heavy wooden doors open onto a cavernous studio with a traditional beamed structure built by local farmers as an addition to a modern courtyard-style house to the rear. With its white walls and floor, exposed brickwork, and industrial lighting, the space has an unexpected New York loft-style feel, positioned as it is in the heart of the Beijing countryside.

A passageway leads off the studio into the heart of the house. Bedrooms shielded by pinewood screens line a corridor which leads into the living room and then to a kitchen. The palette is raw and subdued: warm woods, neutral furnishings, and a blend of antique Chinese and modern European style furniture.

This juxtaposition of the old and the new in modern China is at the heart of Lin Tianmiao's work. "I found it all confusing so I bound things up. Whether the objects are old or modern, the process of wrapping them in thread makes it impossible to use them, denying both their original identity and their ultimate function."

Above: A corridor leads from the studio into a modern courtyard-style family home. Windows on the left look out onto the courtyard; to the right are the family's bedrooms, hidden behind sliding pinewood doors.

Opposite: A huge pinewood tub stands in the corner of the slate-tiled bathroom.

The Candy Factory
From industrial building to creative hub

A 1950s-built former candy factory has emerged as a creative center for Shanghai's art and design industry. The refurbished five-storey building at 210 Taikang Lu, known as the International Artist's Factory (IAF), began life as an experimental project by the Luan district government. It was an instant success and is now home to a growing number of studios, boutiques, and galleries that offer a range of creative services.

Jooi Design has turned its second floor studio, formerly a machine room, into a clean and bright space with painted original concrete floor and towering ceilings. Jooi founder Trine Petersen has filled the 120-square-meter (1,292-sq-ft) space with her collection of retro modern furniture and accessories designed and made in China. She uses tactile materials such as cashmere, silk yarn, ultra-suede, and lacquered elmwood to "fuse the traditions of craftsmanship with a contemporary aesthetic sensibility". At the end of the corridor, online and offline marketers Mailman Ltd have a huge corner studio space complete with Communist worker logo posters, comfy leather sofas, feng shui fish tank, and ping pong table.

Visitors to fourth floor fashion store Tiramisu, owned by Australian retailer Kimberley O'Donnell, encounter a theatrical setting, with frothy Victorian-style organza and silk drapes juxtaposed with a geometric black-and-white floor. It's a cool combination of New York loft and French opulence in a Chinese setting, with racks of fashionable garments designed and made locally. "I aim to produce classic, timeless clothing which is simple, sensual, and elegant," says O'Donnell, who enjoys the grand proportions of her space.

Above: **Retro-modern cashmere and silk pillows and sculptural 'vase-bags', all by Jooi Design.**

Right: **The industrial roots of the International Artist's Factory have been retained in the entrance foyer with an original hoist hanging from the ceiling. To the right, a wooden sign lists the name of every occupant in Chinese characters.**

Above: Each occupant had to renovate the space him- or herself. In Trine Petersen's Jooi Design studio, a former machine room was turned into a light, bright space complete with six-meter-high (20 ft) ceilings and original concrete floor. Inspired by traditional Chinese crafts, Jooi's contemporary furniture and accessories are made using lacquered elmwood, suede, PVC, and silk.

Right: A pair of old wooden doors is juxtaposed against clean-lined furniture with a retro influence. The lounge cube stools are silk on ultra-suede with a silver embroidered disc.

Above: Fashion retailer Kimberley O'Donnell enjoys the grand proportions of her 200-square-meter (2,153-sq-ft) studio. A geometric black-and-white floor combines well with lush burgundy and cream Victorian-style drapes and industrial lighting to form a backdrop to clothes and accessories designed and made in China.

Right: In the corner are furniture classics such as a Mies Barcelona chaise longue. A bamboo ladder painted white functions as a display unit for the lingerie collection.

Above: Industrial Revolution imagery has been updated and used as a company logo as in these ceramic worker figures.

Left: At work and play — Mailman employees move from computer screens to the table tennis table in their open plan office. The space retains a spartan factory feel enlivened by huge red and black communist worker posters. To the left is a mezzanine level, created using industrial metal sheeting.

White Out
Clean, bright, and light

Rising high above the French Concession is the Shanghai home of Richard Lim. His top floor duplex was planned by architect Kenneth Grant Jenkins of JK arQ to let in as much natural light as possible. Once inside, the reason for such spatial planning is clear: it enjoys soaring views over the French Concession district, including Shanghai's famous Clove Garden, an English-style brick and wood villa in sculptural grounds. The villa once belonged to late Qing dynasty viceroy, Li Hongzhang, who gave it to his favorite concu-bine, Dingxiang (Clove), hence its current name.

At night, when the view outside turns into a sea of glittering lights, the city's modern face comes into focus. Shanghai residents like Lim, who is a partner in the homegrown Simply Life chain of décor stores, is one of many entrepreneurs aiming to improve quality of life in China's rapidly growing market.

"We completely reconfigured the apartment," he explains. "We wanted it to be white, bright, and to let in maximum light." On the lower level, doors are kept to a minimum to enhance the flow of space, with rooms divided by raising or lowering the floor. A circu-lar dropped ceiling in the dining room functions in the same way: its curved shape helps to break up the interior's angular lines.

An open stairway leads to the bedroom and study level above, where cleverly installed moving panels substitute walls. Interesting tex-tures, such as lavender stucco paintwork, zebrano wood veneer, white leather, silk, and marble, have been applied to add warmth to the space. Subtle, modern, and glamorous: is this the shape of Shanghai to come?

Above: An open stairway leads to the upper level in Richard Lim's cool white duplex. Marble is used extensively for the floor as it looks clean, bright and helps to reflect light.

Right: The geometric spa-tial proportions produce a calm, understated environ-ment. Lighting is recessed to keep lines clean and accessories are kept to a minimum, focusing on accent pieces such as a reclining Buddha found in Yu Garden antiques market.

Above, left to right:
Delicate chinaware with
goldfish motifs by Grace
Liu of Asianera.
Glassware features
longevity symbols.

Right: The circular dropped
ceiling in the dining room
works to break up the
angular lines. Faded lavender stucco walls add a hint
of color and texture to the
all-white palette. A raised
floor further distinguishes
the dining room from the
main living space. The
contemporary white leather
chairs were custom made
by Simply Life.

Above: The apartment has been designed to be a flexible space. In the upstairs study, the individually lit display shelf unit can be flipped around to reveal a built-in TV. The leather and stainless steel couch also pulls out and can double up as a guest bed.

Above: The first floor master bedroom has a raised floor so that from the bed the eye meets the horizon. On the windows there is a choice of opaque Roman blinds to diffuse the light or fabric covered boards that slide across for total privacy. The bamboo motif bedlinen is by Simply Life.

Left: Silk cushions and ceramic teaware in gold and biscuit shades.

Right: A pile of 1970s cake tins from Hong Kong, collected over the years.

Opposite: Douglas Young's striking commercial art posters are displayed graphically above a sofa. Chosen for their primitive printing techniques that add a certain raw quality, the posters, sourced around the world, include a Mao era propaganda poster and a cigarette advertisement, both found in Shanghai flea markets.

Fusion Central
Raw edges and retro styling

Hong Kong-born and based architect-turned-retailer Douglas Young has always been a style-setter rather than a trend-follower. The man behind the popular G.O.D homeware stores (the name means "to live better" in Cantonese) believes that a global decorative vision, infused with subtle Chinese and Asian characteristics, is the key to contemporary Hong Kong living.

Young aims to bring his message of cross-cultural Orientalism to a wider audience through a celebration of local style. He demonstrates this ethos at work — and at home, which is composed of two 135-square-meter (1,500-sq-ft) apartments knocked into one, in Eastern Mid-Levels above Hong Kong Park. Free-flow of space is key, with walls and doors kept to a minimum. In their place, a series of curved and straight partitions helps to divide the space and make the most of the light that floods in through large front windows.

Young has filled his home with natural, simple materials and furnishings. There is a bamboo kitchen cabinet from Beijing and an antique Chinese writing desk; black leather Philippe Starck armchairs and Diane Arbus black-and-white framed prints; retro European furnishings; and old architectural calligraphy books. Young also looks out for "traditional Chinese items that look modern", which include commercial art posters from a Shanghai flea market, a Mao era propoganda poster, and antique celadonware with ultra-simple shapes that look contemporary. His is a mix-and-match approach: stylish yet artfully casual, put together with an unerring eye.

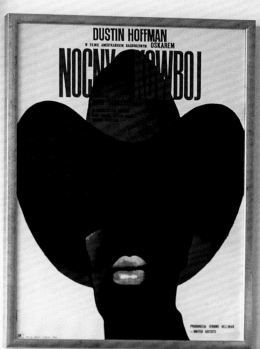

Above: In neutral gear — by combining two 135-square-meter (1,500-sq-ft) apartments into one large living space, the architect produced a characterful home. The living room is a fusion of East-West styles, a mix and match approach that defies location.

Above: In a corner of the living room, the stone façade was found in one of Hong Kong's Hollywood Road antiques stores.

Left: The original 1950s styling of the apartment block has been revisited in the kitchen with its circular wood table and curvaceous country-style benches.

Below: Delicate white and cream ceramicware.

Bottom: A huge plant in a woven pot adds a tropical feel to the bathroom.

Above: In a corner of the room is a 1970s-designed shelf unit containing antique and modern ceramics. Set against the curved wall is a George Nakashima bench; above it hangs a collection of black-and-white photographs including work by Diane Arbus and Victorian photographer Charles Jones.

New Shanghai
Sizzling colors and calligraphic flourishes

Above: **In the corner of the bedroom, a vibrant orange wall acts as a counterfoil to the neutral studio space. On it hangs "Rainbow-B", acrylic on canvas, 2001, by Ann New, which depicts a free-flowing female form. In the foreground is a woven rattan chair and an egg-shaped polyurethane Tato stool by Enrico Baleri and Denis Santachira.**

Right: **A curved wall divides the long, slim interior in two whilst maintaining an open-plan feel. The bedroom, bathroom, and kitchen are on the left and the studio is on the right. A pale palette for the walls and floor ensures minimal visual distraction when the artist is at work.**

For Ann New, the exuberance of modern Shanghai was instrumental in luring her home again. The Shanghai-born artist, known for her vibrant, emotive oils and acrylics — all sizzling color and calligraphic flourishes — studied and lived in Japan, Korea, South Asia, and the United States. Upon returning to the city for an exhibition, she found herself entranced by its rapid transformation and cultural energy and decided to move back.

New is representative of the cosmopolitan influences that are today making her city an exciting place to be. She lives in a loft-like apartment in the French Concession which is as colorful and contemporary as the art she produces. "I wanted a living and working place which were separate but connected," she explains. So she asked architect Benjamin T. Wood (of Wood + Zapata) to come up with the concept design for the 130-square-meter (1,399-sq-ft) space, which was long and slim with a bank of windows at one end only. He devised a curvaceous wall that runs down the middle and effectively splits the space in two, whilst still retaining its open plan feel and light source.

On one side is New's painting studio; on the other the bedroom, bathroom, and kitchen. Furniture is kept to a minimum. "I wanted built-in furniture, it had to be functional," she explains, gesturing to a worktable with a floating concrete top, platform bed, and open rail wardrobe. Whilst the studio is calm and cool, allowing the artworks to take precedence, the bedroom is sensual, with a bright orange wall on one side and a matt black wall on the other. New finds such a wall restful, a break from the color and vigour that infuse the rest of her life.

Above: Artist Ann New at work in her loft-like apartment. She opted for functional built-in furniture throughout the interior such as a large work table with a floating concrete top, anchored on the right side to the wall.

Top left: Behind the bed is "For Once", an acrylic on canvas, 2001, by Ann New.

Bottom left: The bathroom is tucked away behind the dressing area. A large mirrored wall behind the washbasin serves to increase the sense of space.

Above: Looking into the bedroom — the black wall facing the bed was created using a mix of Chinese ink and concrete. New finds it a restful visual break from the vibrant colors surrounding her. The double-railed walk-in closet was designed as an integral part of the room.

Right: Delicate organic porcelainware, designed by Lin Jing.

Far right: A former factory is now a spacious open plan home. The main living room is divided by furniture placement rather than walls. The concrete floor is finished with oil to retain the industrial air. Midnight blue and royal purple velvet curtains draped over a pair of late-Ming horseshoe back armchairs shield the sleeping area from the rest of the room.

Factory Chic
Reshaping an industrial zone

Furniture designer Lin Jing and her film producer husband, Ju Yi, have breathed new life into a disused munitions factory in downtown Beijing. Built by the East Germans in the 1950s and situated in what was once an industrial zone, the building has a stern, utilitarian façade that belies the funky, colorful interior within.

Adhering to the industrial roots of the space, the couple have created an open plan interior, which benefits from rows of windows running along either side. The large, 500-square-meter (5,556 sq ft) space has towering 4.5-meter-high (14.8 ft) ceilings and hard-wearing concrete floors. The upper level is divided into living, dining, working, and sleeping zones with the use of a series of screens, furniture on wheels and voluptuous velvet curtains.

Jing, who trained as a visual artist in both Beijing and Brussels, designed much of the furniture herself. These include sculptural wooden stools, geometric silk and metal screens, glamorous beaded silk lamps, and organic white ceramics. She is talented at seeing the potential in everyday items and injecting creative flair into old things. Hence broken, mismatched factory chairs are bound in sizzling orange, yellow, and turquoise plastic strips to add a dash of quirky humour. An ex-factory metal cabinet from the 1950s with original Maoist slogans enjoys new life as a drinks cabinet. And these happily co-exist alongside antique late Ming chairs, Tibetan carpets, and European designer items, such as Verner Panton's curvaceous Phantom Chair. "People always throw things away but I think you should look, think, and take some time," Lin explains.

Left: Downstairs, a series of rooms function as a display space for Lin Jing's furniture and accessories. A curvaceous pinewood loveseat and Kang table are modern interpretations of traditional Chinese designs. In the corner is a 1950s cabinet, with original Maoist slogans, which was left abandoned in the factory. It is now used as a drinks cabinet.

Above: Old meets new —
adding color to the hallway
is a tall, freestanding silk
beaded lamp designed by
Lin Jing, and an old factory
chair updated with colorful
strips of plastic.

Right: The couple opted for
restaurant style stainless
steel units and trolleys on
wheels to kit out their
kitchen. A bright green
espresso machine sits on
top of a wooden Chinese
table inset with glass.

Right: Around the dining table are abandoned factory chairs bound with colorful plastic tubing in bright yellow, orange, and cream. Behind stands one of the designer's geometric screens, comprising a metal frame inset with colored silk panels.

Art in the City
Traditional exterior, modern interior

On the edge of a moat, a few steps from the entrance to the east wall of Beijing's Forbidden City stands a curved roof *siheyuan* (courtyard house). Originally part of the Imperial Palace, this house used to be owned by an army lieutenant in the Qing Dynasty (1644–1911), then became a factory in the early 1950s, and was later taken over by squatters during the Cultural Revolution (1966–1976).

Now it has been transformed into a modern restaurant, bar and art gallery by Chinese American lawyer, Handel Lee, who bought it together with a group of ten investors. The original structure was in such decrepit state that a new building that aimed to retain the simplicity and elegance of the original had to be built. After five years of bureaucratic delays, The Courtyard finally opened its doors.

From the outside, the house looks like many other restored *siheyuan*, with a traditional sweeping roof, heavy wooden doors, and brass fittings. But inside it is full-on modern. The large square restaurant boasts track lighting, wooden floors, white walls, and a vaulted solarium glass roof that covers the actual courtyard.

A small foot bridge crosses an open well in the center of the restaurant, through which guests can peer down at the art gallery in the basement. This device visually links the two spaces. Since its opening in 1996, The Courtyard Gallery has become a center for contemporary Chinese art worldwide. Its director, Meg Maggio, who represents artists such as the Gao Brothers, Guo Wei and Guo Jin, Chen Wenji, and Lin Tianmiao, says: "The art scene here [Chinese art world] is innovative, creative, and inspired; similar to 1950s New York."

Above: This 150-year-old *siheyuan* house near the Forbidden City was completely renovated during its transformation into an art gallery and restaurant. The entranceway features traditional sweeping tiled roof, burnished red doors, and brass fittings; inside it is light, bright, and modern.

Opposite: The Courtyard art gallery is located on the lower level and offers rotating exhibitions of contemporary Chinese art, aiming to bring Chinese artists to a local audience. A small bridge traverses the middle of the restaurant, allowing diners to peer down at the exhibition below.

Left: White floors, pale woodwork, and a glass and steel roof create a calming, light interior. On display in the gallery are works by independent female artist Lin Tianmiao, who uses thread to bind everyday objects, including bicycles and tree branches.

Below: A photographic installation and thread-bound bicycle by Lin Tianmiao, which plays on urban residents' perceptions of the countryside.

Above: Inside, the restaurant occupies the central square courtyard, which would have originally been open to the elements. Bamboo matting overlays the glass roof to protect the interior from the sun. The large windows overlooking the Forbidden City ensure spectacular views — especially at night.

Above: Contemporary art is displayed in the dining room — on the wall are three panels from the "Abstract Landscape Series", 1999, by Shanghai artist Qiu Deshu who produces collages using traditional Xuanzhi paper. Xuanzhi is made from sandalwood bark and rice stalks and, due to its high quality, has long been popular with Chinese painters.

Zen Hideaway
A calming retreat in the city

Architect Dan Lee of AB Concept lives in the heart of Hong Kong's neon-clad shopping and entertainment district of Causeway Bay. Outside his home, people throng the streets day and night, so it comes as no surprise that he chose to turn his 88-square-meter (950-sq-ft) apartment into a serene retreat.

Built in the 1960s, Lee's apartment enjoys a sense of space and character seldom found in newer, box-like Hong Kong developments. Lee stained the original wood floor dark brown to achieve a glossy lacquer-like finish. For extra atmosphere, he replaced the overhead lighting with soft spotlights and freestanding lamps. Lee describes his home as "international with a Chinese flavor", whereby simple forms, geometric lines, and regular proportions form the backdrop for a Zen-like blend of furnishings and accessories. A contemporary own-design sofa, side table, and retro-inspired striped carpet (under Lee's retail homeware label, Ovo) share space with cowhide cushions, a Christian Liaigre stool, and select pieces of Chinese furniture. "I like to take plain and simple things and mix them with other objects to create another character," he explains.

Lee displays a commitment to harmony not just visually but sensually too. "I didn't purposefully design the interior with feng shui in mind," he explains. "But it is good to have plants and water around and to keep your interior simple." Single-stem orchids, bowls filled with floating lilies, candles, and incense burners of all shapes and sizes add a meditative air to the space. It is a cocoon in an increasingly hectic world.

Top: Next to an antique cabinet stands a Thai crackle-glaze ceramic bowl. Above hangs a black-and-white photograph of traditional Chinese gardens.

Above: Natural elements are key — lily pads, goldfish, and floating candles.

Right: Lee's 40-year-old apartment (old in Hong Kong terms) is filled with a retro chic mix of modern European and classic Chinese furniture. The focus is on "plain and simple designs which, when mixed with other things, take on a new character".

Above: Geometric shapes and balanced proportions lead a modern Oriental feel to the living room. Lee kept the furniture low-level to make the most of the compact space. The Ovo sofa, which slots under a contemporary cherrywood and steel altar table, is based on the traditional daybed concept.

In the foreground is a stool by French designer Christian Liaigre; the barcode wool carpet in plum, cream, and green retro stripes lifts the subtle interior.

Above: The master bedroom is a soothing sanctuary in muted tones, which is ideal for relaxation. "It doesn't have to be expensive; most of this isn't but it all has simple forms, geometric lines, and nice proportions."

Above: Lee has always been interested in antique Chinese furniture and pottery, "especially that related to Buddhism". In the corner of the dining room stands a recessed leg table that functions as an altar.

Feng Shui Friendly
The circulation of chi

This 600-square-meter (6,458-sq-ft) house is located in Kowloon Tong, a 1960s-built luxury residential district in Hong Kong. When the owners decided to give their home a facelift after ten years, they engaged interior architects Caroline Ma and Jason Yung of Jason and Caroline Design. Being firm advocates of feng shui, which refers to living in harmony with the environment to enable good energy (*chi*) to promote well-being and good fortune, the owners wanted an interior that was both visually pleasing and in line with feng shui dictates. So Ma and Yung worked closely with a feng shui master.

"Many designers are reluctant to work with feng shui masters as they believe good design and good feng shui cannot co-exist," explains Ma. "In this project we wanted to prove otherwise." The location and orientation of the different rooms and furniture, and of the five ancestral shrines, were predefined. Ma based her design concept on the circulation of *chi*. "According to feng shui, *chi* carries energy. It allows the house to breathe. So we decided to emphasize the circular form and eliminate as many corners as possible to allow the smooth flow of energy." Thus undulating curves are everywhere: a circular spiral staircase; smoothened wall corners; a quarter circle balcony, the shower cubicle; even a curved walk-in closet in the master bedroom.

To further accentuate the curves, and to reflect the history of the house and the owners, who were married in the 1960s, Ma opted for a modern interpretation of a retro furnishing scheme, combining classic pieces with contemporary designs. The result is a cyber-white setting that is as much of the future as it is of the past.

Opposite: **The glamorous curves of this gleaming duplex owe as much to feng shui principles as they do to the owners' love of retro design. Energy giving *chi* is funneled up the curvaceous stairwell (see above) with the help of a six-meter-high (20 ft) dappled chandelier. The stairwell is situated in the center of the residence and links the ground floor with the upper bedroom floor. Raised and dropped ceilings inset with lighting are based on a geometric grid to help to balance the curves.**

Above: A '60s-style break-fast bar complements the open kitchen.

Right: The circular dining table (a round table symbolizes heavenly blessings) seats ten and is ideal for traditional Chinese banqueting. Bleached white wood floors, a cushioned wall, and opaque glass panels add textural interest whilst retaining a minimal feel.

Opposite: In the cavernous living room, a large semi-circular Minotti sofa echoes the circular theme. The emphasis on rounded forms eliminates as many corners as possible and allows a smooth flow of energy. White marble floors also help to usher in as much light as possible. Retro patterned curtains enhance the '60s look. (Photo by Jason + Caroline Architecture)

Opposite: Even the walk-in closet is curved, which proves as practical as it is aesthetically-pleasing — it allows the owner to see all her clothes at a glance. (photo by Jason + Caroline Architecture)

Above: A semi-sunken Jacuzzi tub and a glass shower cubicle continue the circular theme in the bathroom.

Cool Customer
A series of unfurling vistas

Architect Ed Ng created a serene family environment on the secluded coastal headland of Chung Hom Kok on Hong Kong's south side. Comprising two houses knocked into one, the impressive 743-square-meter (8,000-sq-ft) interior covers four levels, complete with a spacious terrace and negative edge swimming pool. The space has an open quality: there are few doors with rooms divided by partitioned and cut-out walls, which allow tantalizing glimpses of rooms beyond.

"The owner wanted the interior based on a Chinese garden-type design with 'bridges,' which allowed one view and then another," explains Ng. "So we designed it so that you don't see everything at once; it's a very Chinese way of approaching spatial design."

The stairways are an integral part of the design and are balustrade-free to enhance the free-flowing feel. "The entry staircase is the beginning of the experience of the home. I wanted to make a statement so made it out of 15-cm (6-in) solid stone," says Ng. Throughout the house, the materials used are tasteful and understated, with cool limestone and walnut wood floors, plain white walls, floating shelves and rich textures to add interest.

"I always try to have a feature wall in every room but white is the common language for all areas. A distinctive backdrop, such as metallic bronze, white leather, or macassar ebony, gives it character." Geometric and minimal, this precisely designed space is the epitome of modern luxury: quiet, understated, and elegant.

Above: Architect Ed Ng reworked what was a circular entrance foyer into an open space with geometric stairway. Made of solid limestone, the stairs were designed with built-in ledges to display ceramics and sculptures.

Opposite: Adding light to the entrance hall is a floor-to-ceiling mirror with a Macassar ebony frame. In front of it is a modern scroll-inspired bench. From the ceiling hangs a light by Andrée Putman for Baccarat.

Left: Detail of black-and-white ceramic dinnerware by Ovo Living.

Opposite: The staircases are an integral part of the interior and are balustrade-free to enhance the flowing spatial proportions. Above a solid pine table is the depiction of a Tang dynasty poet, "Hsieh Ling Yun reciting poetry," by Fan Zheng, a mainland artist.

Above and right: On each floor, doors have been kept to a minimum; instead spaces are divided by cut-out partitioning walls, which reflect the design of traditional Chinese gardens, allowing unfurling vistas and glimpses into spaces. On the first floor is a family relaxation area (above) with a white leather padded feature wall and a dining area (right) with a bronze metallic fiber wall.

Above: Natural textures —
in the guest bathroom,
a white ceramic country-
style sink rests on a solid
oak bench.

Opposite: Zen-like simplicity defines the tatami guest
room, which is enlivened
by the brushed metal fiber
feature wall. Rice paper
blinds diffuse the light.

Above: The beige, purple, and slate palette in the master bedroom provides a more feminine feel. The bamboo motif carpet, with four stalks to represent the four family members, was designed by the owner and produced by Ovo Living. Horizontal strips of carpet divided by stainless steel trims cover the rear wall.

Opposite: The *en suite* bathroom features a free-standing tub by Philippe Starck. Wood is key — the wall is covered with straight grain walnut; the floor of walnut planks. Recessed and spot lighting add warmth to the relaxing space.

Neighborhood Watch
A fresh look at the Chinese aesthetic

Sai Ying Pun lies to the West of Central on Hong Kong Island —
just a few minutes by car from the bustling business district but
a world apart in terms of atmosphere. Here, in the heart of this
old-style neighborhood filled with jumbled shops and street side
restaurants, live Cecilia Bengsston and Harald Steinbrecher.

Saying a firm "no" to glitzy Hong Kong towerblock living,
the Swedish couple chose to decorate their 56-square-meter
(600-sq-ft) home in a 40-year-old building to reflect a slice of Hong
Kong history. In keeping with traditional shophouse-like structures,
the layout is long and narrow, with rooms stretching backwards
from the street. Using a simple, all-white palette for the floor, ceiling,
and walls, Bengsston scoured the area for decorative Chinese
items with timeless appeal. The result is a fresh, feminine interior
that breathes new life into what many would consider everyday
items: tiny bamboo stools, woven wicker baskets, pink and mint
green silks, and 1920s painted glass mirrors. "My guidelines are
that you have to use local products. It has to be a neighorbood
thing," explains Bengsston.

Her artistic flair comes into the mix too. When living in Shanghai,
Bengsston began collecting old 1960s sepia and black-and-white
Chinese family photographs that she found in the flea markets. She
continued her collection in Hong Kong and has since used computer
imaging techniques to enlarge some of the prints onto oversized
paper scrolls, which now hang from her living room wall. A creative
interpretation of the way life used to be in a country close to her heart.

Top: Next to the old-style
entrance doors is a minia-
ture wooden chair and a pink
lotus-shaped paper lantern.

Above: On the wall, a
famous Chinese poem, "In
the Quiet Night" by Li Bai.

Right: The oversized scrolls
on the living room wall are
designed and produced
by Cecilia Bengsston. The
woollen carpet depicting a
lakeside pagoda is from
Xinjiang province.

Left: A pair of white sofas provides the bare bones of Bengsston's serene white decorative scheme. Accessories include Chinese antiques and memorabilia such as 1920s painted glass mirrors, pink and mint green silks, and woven baskets, all sourced in Hong Kong.

Above: The apartment is long and narrow, stretching backwards from the living room on the street side. The country-style kitchen is located at the bottom of a small set of stairs, sandwiched between the bedroom and the study.

Above: Splashes of color brighten up the all-white study. On the far wall hangs a pair of textiles by modernist Swedish artist Olle Baertling.

Left: On the wall, a Chinese name 'chop', or signature seal, has been printed repetitively. Chops have been used since the Sung dynasty. They are engraved by hand, pressed into a red ink paste made from cinnabar, and usually stamped on a painting or document.

Above: In the bedroom, embroidered red silk Chinese cushion covers and a hanging made from a red silk scroll add visual energy. The wooden stool was painted white to match the paintwork and bedspread.

Echoes of the Past

As China rushes into the future, much of its traditional architecture is being destroyed. As city planners rush to improve the infrastructure and house a rapidly growing population, *hutongs* (maze-like alleyways), and *siheyuan* (courtyard houses) in Beijing, and *longtangs* (lane houses) and art deco apartment blocks in Shanghai are being leveled to make way for gleaming high-rises. But there is hope on the horizon. The calls for preservation are gradually becoming louder as conservationists, scholars, artists, and professionals make a concerted effort to help save the cities' cultural heritages.

It is also becoming increasingly popular, among stylish urbanites who have the design sense and the commitment, to restore and live in atmospheric structures, including Qing courtyard houses and 1930s art deco apartments. Against a traditional backdrop, decorative elements — from Mao era collectibles to vibrant modern art — are introduced to create a contemporary living space that is traditional Chinese, but with a twist. In Hong Kong too, whispers of a bygone era remain in gems such as a 1920s garage and 1950s apartment blocks which blend East-West influences with innovation and flair.

Above: In the reception area of restaurant T8 is an ultra slim fish tank inset into a galvanized metal façade.

Right: Upstairs, the private club lounge offers a relaxed ambience with Chinese accents. The room features a soaring ceiling with traditional timber pillars to support the roof. Furnishings and accessories include easy chairs and sofas in neutral shades, an antique daybed, and oversized birdcages.

Shikumen Style
A hybrid form of East-West architecture

Hip new entertainment district Xintiandi has changed the face of Shanghai. Living proof of the city's ability to reinvent itself, Xintiandi is a rapidly growing 50-hectare (124-acre) (on completion) complex of shops, bars, restaurants, apartments, and commercial spaces which stands where rows of 19th century *shikumen* houses — a hybrid form of East-West architecture unique to Shanghai — used to be.

What makes Xintiandi different is that it has, in part, attempted to retain a portion of Shanghai's architectural heritage. Hong Kong developer, Shui On Properties, restored — or part restored — two square blocks of old houses, which included the site that was the first meeting place of the Chinese Communist Party.

Designed by Boston architects Wood + Zapata, Xintiandi, which literally means "new earth and sky," is wildly popular. Crowds throng the narrow streets day and night. One of the most popular spots is T8, a luxurious bar and restaurant downstairs and private club upstairs, which coolly combines a *shikumen* structure with subdued Zen-like furnishings.

The interior designers of the project reflect the internationalism of Shanghai today: upstairs is the work of Indonesian designer Jaya Ibrahim, known for his spatial organization and sensitivity to local culture, while downstairs is by Tokyo-based Spin Design Studio. Whilst it is obvious that two hands have been at work here, the styles are complementary and the resultant wooden beamed ceiling, exposed tiled walls, iron latticework, and textured contemporary soft furnishings produce an understated environment that is relaxing and inviting.

Left: Many of the bars, restaurants and shops in the Xintiandi development are based in restored or partially-restored *shikumen* houses, built by foreign developers in the mid-19th century. Here the bar area in T8 restaurant retains a raw edge with exposed grey slate tiling and metal lattice-work. The painting on the rear wall is by Pang Yong Jie, a Shangdong artist whose voluptuous portraits are inspired by perceptions of beauty during the Tang dynasty (AD 618–907).

Clockwise from top left:
Latticework features traditional Chinese patterns such as cracked ice (originally found in Ming dynasty window designs).

Neutral furnishings with orange accents add energy to the subtle Chinese-Asian décor in this room.

An art deco inspired desk in the upper level reception area.

Dark woods and clean lines in the private dining room.

Heart of Stone
Residing in a 1920s garage

Above: The cosy mustard yellow guest bedroom, with white linens and antique French iron bed is located on a mezzanine level. It is accessed through hinged doors inset with panels of *cha geng* (tea-colored mirror), which can be pulled across for privacy.

Right: The ground floor is predominantly open plan and designed to retain the original character of the space. The two-meter-thick (7-ft) stone walls are left exposed and painted white; the downstairs floor is covered with black slate. Above the dining area, an industrial sheet metal walkway with wrought-iron detailing leads to two guest bedrooms; to the right is a stainless steel kitchen.

On shady Kotewall Road on the fringes of Mid-Levels, a slice of Hong Kong's architectural history remains. The only property of its kind in Hong Kong today, the former 1923 three-car garage-cum-mews-house was turned into a hip urban living space by American lawyer, CJ Wysocki, and his wife Gloria. The 270-square-meter (3,000 sq ft) interior now comprises a two-storey space with six-meter-high (20 ft) ceilings, two-meter-thick (7-ft) stone walls, an internal six-meter-high spiral staircase, and industrial sheet metal walkways. Downstairs, three double doors in black sheet metal remain along the building's facade — one functions as the main entrance door.

It is a calm, cool interior with a quasi-ecclesiastical feel. The space is largely open plan: downstairs are living and dining areas, an industrial style kitchen, and two guest bedrooms on a mezzanine level. Upstairs is a cosier living room and a master bedroom tucked away on a curved balcony above.

Current tenants, Kristin Flanagan and fiancé Eoin O'Shea, have furnished the place with a chic mix of antique Chinese furniture, classic retro pieces from New York and Paris flea markets, and 1950s designer items. Flanagan admits to being "quite a minimalist," and whilst her possessions come from a variety of sources, they are linked by a commitment to clean lines and classic style. Hence a Le Corbusier chaise longue stands alongside a Shanghainese dining table and chairs; colored glassware from New York is juxtaposed against a bronze Buddha from Chiang Mai; and a pair of 1950s leather armchairs from Paris sits well opposite a traditional Chinese birdcage.

Opposite: The interior has a calm, almost ecclesiastical air, thanks to its soaring ceilings. In one corner, a spiral staircase leads up to the loft-style living room. To the right hangs a tall bird-cage from Kowloon's bird market. The antique Qing dynasty canopy bed is covered in vibrant Chinese silk colored cushions.

Left: The master bedroom is located on a curved balcony above the upstairs living room, accessed via an open industrial metal stairway painted red. "It's cosy, like a little nook," explains Flanagan. The arched doorway below leads onto a private terrace. The industrial fan by the door was once used in the kitchens of Hong Kong's Foreign Correspondents Club.

Below: Upstairs is a loft-style space in which a pair of custom-made elmwood trunks works as a coffee table, with a collection of glass spheres found in Shenzhen, Sydney, and New Zealand displayed on top. On the windowsill sits a bronze Buddha from Chiang Mai, Thailand.

Au Naturel
A sanctuary high on The Peak

High on The Peak, one of Hong Kong's most exclusive residential areas, a low rise 1950s-built apartment block offers panoramic views of Hong Kong Island South and the outlying islands beyond. It is in this atmospheric location that designer Lisbeth Beise and her husband Carter have chosen to make their home.

The 234-square-meter (2,600 sq-ft) interior is a celebration of emotive design. "I don't like to over-intellectualize. I know the elements I love and if I love them they work almost anywhere. I feel it inside," explains Beise, who believes it is important that a space feels like a home as she then can recharge in it.

The key to creating such a sanctuary, Beise believes, is to bring the outside indoors. "I base a lot of my designs on nature." To this end, she has used a natural palette of greens, greys, and faded lavender, with plants in every room. Windows are covered with bamboo blinds draped with voluminous lengths of nylon parachute material to allow maximum light to filter through. Textures are also of paramount importance, as revealed in Beise's modern designs of circular cushions covered in Chinese silk and tassels, and a chequer board made with a lacquer base and turquoise beads.

The serene space is also a collector's paradise, filled with treasured pieces from China, South America, and Japan, plus own-design items inspired by Chinese culture. It is a mixture of old and new, decoratively arranged in surprising and innovative ways. As Beise explains, "The eye must keep moving."

Top: **Lisbeth Beise has put a modern spin on a Qing dynasty bamboo vest by mounting it in a clear Perspex display case.**

Above: **A new take on a traditional game. Beise made the beads out of turquoise and housed them in a burnished lacquer box.**

Right: **An east-facing 'natural' living room. The oil painting is by Fang Chenkong, a Chinese artist based in Brazil. The wooden door is a Koradoa, a sliding storage house door from Japan. The table-light base is made of a wooden fish trap from Northern Brazil; the coffee table is made of two Chinese chests topped with glass.**

Clockwise from top left:
A small bamboo country-style chair and delicate paper cube lights by French designers Tsé & Tsé.
Decorative arrangements of old and new: a Taiwanese statue is draped with beads from Nagaland.
A multi-drawered Korean medicine cabinet.
Circular cushions based on designs from old arm-chairs have been updated using dragonfly motif silk, coins, and tassels.

Above: The master bedroom, with its faded lavender walls, is a calming oasis. Voluminous yellow drapes made of nylon parachute material are held back by traditional Chinese mosquito net hooks; behind, bamboo blinds gently diffuse the light. From the ceiling hangs a large antique Chinese birdcage from Zhuhai.

Precious Jewel
Burnished red and Beijing green

International jewelry and fashion accessory designer Jehanne de Biolley came to China in search of inspiration and found the perfect location for a research base and workshop in the form of a Ming dynasty courtyard building in central Beijing. Rows of bamboo planted in the peaceful courtyard cast shadows into the cavernous interior, with its burnished red pillars and soaring four-meter (13-ft) high ceilings.

It is an ideal environment for nourishing and stimulating creativity. "Although I have a showroom in London, I spend a lot of time in China now as many of my materials, such as agates, pearls, and jade are sourced here. I am also interested in traditional Chinese workmanship, which inspires me. I could work anywhere but choose China as there is still an energy here that is raw and spontaneous."

The space was previously used as a factory, as is evident from the industrial piping that still remains. De Biolley has retained its spacious proportions — "I like the bareness of the space" — adding 1950s-style furnishings, such as green modular leather furniture combined with antique pieces and contemporary Chinese art. "Everything is made in China," she explains. "I call the sofa Beijing green as it is in harmony with the bamboo outside."

The setting offers a blend of comfort, practicality, and fantasy, which is experienced on balmy summer evenings when friends eat alfresco in the courtyard, accompanied by birdsong and the muted hooting of car horns. Secluded and achingly beautiful, it is an evocative blend of ancient China and modern design.

Top: Rows of bamboo trees in the courtyard gently filter the sunlight and provide a soothing backdrop to the pale green living room. Industrial heating pipes line the walls; on the chair is a fabric throw from Xinjiang province, colored with vegetable dyes.

Right: Made in China — de Biolley retained the 1950s concrete flooring and used latticework panels, green leather modular furniture, and a painting by Zhang Gong (from Beijing's The Courtyard Gallery) to add visual energy to the spacious interior.

Left: A row of burnished red pillars runs along the courtyard side of the room. A shrine is at the end; to the left is a Beijing-style altar table with an old gramophone on top. The commanding proportions of the space were a key element in defining Biolley's decorative scheme.

Opposite, clockwise from top left: Jehanne de Biolley's jewelry, inspired by her life in China.

A chunky, Qing dynasty red lacquer wedding cabinet features butterfly-shaped metal hardware. Regarded as an auspicious symbol, the butterfly denotes beauty, elegance, and happiness, while two butterflies symbolize happiness in marriage or relationships. In the foreground, a mannequin is draped in necklaces made of quartz, agates, pearls, and shells.

Red brick, concrete, and deep green — with its original wooden framework, the bathroom is a contemplative space. Light seeps in through the sloping glass roof above.

Hutong Hip
Colorful Qing dynasty courtyard living

Belgian banker Juan van Wassenhove lives in a 150-year-old Qing dynasty courtyard house in the heart of Beijing, near the Forbidden City. Such enclosed, one-storey quadrangles, or *siheyuan*, were common in old Beijing, but are today being bulldozed into oblivion to make way for wider roads and modern high-rises.

Van Wassenhove's house is accessed through *hutongs*, Beijing's signature winding lanes that used to number in the thousands. These lanes still offer glimpses of a community-oriented life played out in public areas.

As with most *siheyuans*, Van Wassenhove's 300-square-meter (3,228-sq-ft) home comprises inward facing rooms set around a courtyard — or, in his case, two courtyards. Designed according to the rules of feng shui and the Confucian tenets of order and hierarchy, it offers refuge from the cacophony of modern day Beijing. The inward facing design also protects residents from harsh winter winds and summer dust storms.

Decoratively, Van Wassenhove draws on the treasures of old Beijing to create a colorful interior. These include 1950 vintage black-and-white photographs from flea markets and retro armchairs from villas once occupied by Communist Party cadres; Cultural Revolution memorabilia and Xinjiang carpets; an antique latticework canopy bed, and tiny green wooden *hutong* chairs.

Seated in his courtyard, Van Wassenhove says, "Here I am in the center of the city yet feel as though I am in the countryside. I don't have to escape at the weekends if I have here."

Top: Lining the windowsill are flea market purchases and a modern ceramic pop art tile.

Above: Fun collectibles — Tintin comic books.

Opposite: The main reception room, flanked by courtyards, contains a 1950s armchair, a Ming-style *ji-chi mu* (chicken wing wood) canopy bed, a carpet from Xinjiang province, and a mulberry paper lamp by Japanese designer Isamu Noguchi.

Above: Latticework screens divide the rectangular reception room into living and dining areas. In traditional Chinese houses, such screens were frequently used as partition walls to divide up the floor space. On the rear wall hangs a work by artist Ai An. Oversized cushions add comfort to the textured slate floor.

Right: A reproduction Cultural Revolution 'Mao girl' and an old-style telephone.

Bottom: A carved stone door base stands at the entrance to the reception area.

Below: Detail of a traditional ceramic drum stool with protective lion motif.

Right: The main courtyard functions as an extension of the house, a place to cultivate plants and flowers and to interact with nature. Against a wall stand pieces of green-painted wooden *hutong* furniture.

The Last Emperor
A strong, sensual design approach

Cultural influences spanning the globe come together in CJ and Gloria Wysocki's spacious duplex on Hong Kong island. "We were thinking Christian Liaigre meets the Last Emperor, or Armani Casa meets Issey Miyake," notes Wysocki.

The two-storey, 306-square-meter (3,400-sq-ft) penthouse is beautifully proportioned and decorated. The floors are linked by an iron spiral staircase in the corner. The Wysockis substantially reworked the space to produce a chic living and dining zone down-stairs and a cosy bedroom–relaxation area upstairs. *Ban-ma mu* (zebra wood) veneer has been used extensively, as has sisal flooring, dark stained wood furniture, and industrial-style stainless steel. "We tried to take the strong sensual elements that we liked and blend them together in a practical way," says CJ. Soft furnishings stick mostly to a palette of matt gold, bronze, cream, and slate for a hint of understated but user-friendly glamor.

Most of the furniture and furnishings were sourced in Hong Kong, although trips around the region have yielded some interesting finds. Playful elements, such as crystal chandeliers sprayed matt black, huge *cha geng* (tea mirror) panels in the dining room and gold-leaf painted alcoves, add further interest to the space. Poster-sized ances-tral photographs, both Chinese and American, reflecting the couple's heritage, hang from the walls in the hallway and in the study.

Overall, the look is simple, precise, and focused: the key to suc-cess when blending different cultural elements. "Otherwise it could be more like Empress Dowager meets Laura Ashley," laughs the owner.

Above: **Enlarged sepia-toned family portrait photographs line the walls of the corridor, which connects the dining room to the study and living rooms. A marble Burmese Buddha (over 100 years old) sits in an alcove lined with gold leaf paper. From the ceiling hangs a crystal chan-delier which has been spray painted matt black.**

Opposite: **The spiral stair-case in the corner of the entranceway was installed by the original developer of the 28-year-old building. It works to link the two floors. "We like to look for something unusual in the context of the city we are in," explains CJ.**

Above: The second living room was designed for relaxation, with its navy sofa, dark shutters, and burning incense. Flanking the sofa is a pair of solid silver dragon candlesticks from Jakarta; on the wall hangs a black-and-white photograph of Gloria's great grandmother and mother.

Below: In the dining room, a large solid silver dragon candlestick from Jakarta stands on top of a Qing dynasty blackwood altar table.

Bottom: Mirror-fronted bathroom cabinets increase the sense of space. An opaque glass brick wall behind the bath allows the room to explode with light in the day.

Right: Behind a 19th century table from Southern China is a row of floor-to-ceiling cabinets made of *ban-ma mu* veneer.

Twenties with a Twist
Art deco inspirations

The late 1920s was a time of prolific apartment building in Shanghai, with new construction techniques paving the way for towering art deco edifices. Buildings such as the Peace Hotel and The Customs House on the Bund and Grosvenor House in the French Concession may be famous examples of the genre but they are certainly not alone. Shanghai is filled with lesser-known buildings — many in advanced states of disrepair — which enable the city to stake its claim as having one of the highest concentrations of art deco style buildings in the world.

The Gresham, located on Huai Hai Zhong Lu (which was once Avenue Joffre), was built in the late 1920s by French architectural firm Leonard, Veyssyre, and Kruze. A Chinese-Polish joint venture, it combines a utilitarian air with whispers of faded glamor. Christopher and Samantha Torrens, together with their daughter Maya, chose a 150-square-meter (1,616 sq ft) apartment in The Gresham as their home. "Shanghai is one of the few cities in Asia with a tradition of art deco architecture — something we only began to appreciate when we came to live here five years ago," says Christopher. "We really felt that we wanted to live in a home that was uniquely Shanghainese."

To furnish the space the Torrens' combed Shanghai's flea markets, factories, antique stores, and custom furniture makers to produce a decorative scheme that complements the apartment's art deco lines. "We wanted to keep an art deco feel to the flat but not to make it completely so," explains Samantha. "So we mixed both Chinese and Western pieces while still trying to retain a Shanghainese feel."

Opposite: A sheer curtain and latticework screen separates the living room from the master bedroom. An antique cabinet with circular metal hinges further defines the two spaces.

Above: The Ming-style hoof-footed elmwood bed is based on a classic *kang* table design. To the side, a cream silk 1930s lotus lamp acts as a bedside lamp.

Sense of Soul
East-West influences, full of feminine flair

Above: Made in China — in the main living room, soft shades of lilac and green have been used for the sofas, door hanging, scatter cushions, and lampshades. The light and airy design is reflective of the building's Mediterranean roots. "I like to take the old and use it in a new way," says Virginie Fournier.

Right: All all-white palette — a pair of white armchairs flanks a Chinese trunk in a reading area at the end of the long living room. Bamboo blinds protect the interior from the strong sunlight.

Amid acres of landscaped gardens in the heart of Shanghai's French Concession district stands a 400-square-meter (4,306-sq-ft) Mediterranean style house built in the 1930s. One of 28 villas of differing Western styles, it was built as part of the Xing Guo Hotel (now the Radisson Plaza Xing Guo Shanghai). Visitors to these peaceful grounds will find it hard to believe that they are in the middle of the city. Even Chairman Mao held this urban oasis in high esteem — he used to stay in nearby Villa Number One (they are all numbered) when in town.

The villa now houses homeware designer and retailer Virginie Fournier and her family. "We love it; it is such a beautiful space," she explains. "It is full of light on the second floor which is rare for most old Shanghai houses and it has a huge garden. It also has a soul."

The villa's spacious proportions have been enhanced by Fournier's sensitive decorative scheme, which mixes her own design furniture and soft furnishings (under the label Shanghai Trio) with Chinese antiques and modern accessories. The light and airy palette reflects the villa's Mediterranean roots: white wood and paintwork, soft green and lilac upholstery, silk lampshades, and a country-style entrance hall.

"Except for the books, some lights, and some vases, everything has been purchased or made in Shanghai or China," Fournier explains. "The most interesting thing for me is that the Chinese shapes are often really contemporary. I take time to choose or make them, each piece has a history or a story behind it."

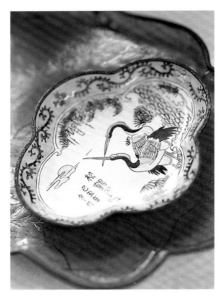

Above: Delicate painted boxes and trays feature Chinese pastoral imagery.

Right: The perfect playroom — lime green, orange, and pink add flair to the room belonging to Virginie Fournier's daughter. A painted kite hangs on the wall; paper lanterns dangle from a bamboo ladder.

Above: A traditional arched window softens the lines of the dining room. A bookcase made of square boxes of differing sizes and proportions is filled with books and flea market finds. Fournier scours local warehouses, small shops, and the city's street markets hunting for items with a contemporary feel.

Right: In a corner of the bedroom — collections of leather trunks and boxes.

Right: A pair of Chinese trunks provides an end-of-bed display area for collectibles including a test-tube vase, lacquer boxes, and mini leather trunk. The bedlinen with Chinese motifs is by Shanghai Trio.

Soho Living
Rich colors and warm textures in the city

Compact inner city living may be a fact of life in Hong Kong, but lack of space doesn't have to mean lack of inspiration, as Susan Paolini and Larry Quek's bijou city pad shows. Located in the busy restaurant and bar district of SoHo (South of Hollywood Road), the abode reflects the cosmopolitan lifestyle of its owners, who split their time between Hong Kong, Beijing and New York. It may be just 45 square meters (500 sq ft) in size, but the lush interior, designed by Alec Stuart of Alexander Stuart Designs, is reminiscent of a New York loft in its feeling of openness.

"I love the ease of being able to walk about and feel like you're still moving," says Paolini. A small open kitchen nestles by the front door; the living room extends horizontally into a dining room; and the bedroom lies to the left, partitioned off by a Qing dynasty screen.

Here in the bedroom, vibrant colors, warm textures, and unlacquered Chinese furniture prove an ideal mix. The rich orange walls of the bedroom offset a chocolate-brown suede covered bed and the carved screen. In the living room, the furniture provides the colour: a purple Chesterfield-style sofa, sizzling lime and yellow lampshades, bright silk cushions, and modern Chinese art. To top it off is a saltwater tropical fish tank that Stuart neatly incorporated into an ashwood veneer bookcase. Apart from its positive feng shui connotations — water brings abundance and moving water indicates moving money — the tank provides hours of aesthetic enjoyment for the others. "It's beautiful. We can spend ages just sitting here and staring at it."

Top: In the bedroom, rich orange walls are an ideal foil for the chocolate brown, pigskin suede bed, which is covered with Asian silks.

Above: Detail of a scroll by artist Li Jin hanging in the living room. It depicts a Beijing banquet.

Opposite: A latticework Qing dynasty elmwood screen functions as a sliding door to the bedroom — it can be closed for privacy or opened to increase the sense of space in the apartment. The unlacquered tapered cabinet was purchased in Beijing.

Above: In the open plan living and dining room, walls are neutral and floors are made of textured grey slate. Color is provided by a two-meter (8-ft) purple velvet Chesterfield-style sofa.

Above: A 273-liter (60-gallon) saltwater tropical fish tank has been built into the ashwood veneer bookcase in the corner of the living room. It has a slate backdrop, which echoes that used for the living room floor. A pair of Chinese butterfly stools made using wood from an old door sourced in Beijing act as bar stools. Behind the midnight blue armchair hangs a scroll by Li Jin which depicts a Beijing banquet.

Acknowledgements

Thank you to Meg Maggio and Shaway Yeh in Beijing and to Choon in Shanghai for your help, enthusiasm and introductions. Thank you to all the architects, designers and homeowners who feature in this book: your imagination and originality are inspiring.

AB Concept Limited
G/F 32-33 Sau Wa Fong
Wanchai, Hong Kong
Tel: 852 2525 2428
Fax: 852 2854 1038
info@abconcept.com.hk
www.abconcept.com.hk

Jason Caroline Design
6/F 31 Wyndham Street
Hong Kong
Tel: 852 9027 2332
Fax: 852 2893 4061
jas_car@hotmail.com

Alexander Stuart Designs
5/F 15B Wellington Street
Hong Kong
Tel: 852 2526 6155
Fax: 852 2548 9410
astuart@pacific.net.hk

Douglas Young
GOD Ltd, 48 Hollywood
Road, Hong Kong
Tel: 852 2544 5615
Fax: 852 2543 9377
www.god.com.hk

The CourtYard Gallery
95 Donghuamen Dajie
Dongcheng District
Beijing 100006
Tel: 86 10 6526 8882
Fax: 86 10 6526 8880
Info@CourtYard-Gallery.com
www.courtyard-gallery.com

China Art Archives &
Warehouse, PO Box 43
Beijing 100102
Tel: 86 10 8456 5152
Fax: 86 10 8456 5154
caaw@public.gb.com.cn
www.archivesandware-
house.com

Redstone Industrie Co Ltd
18-20/F Tower B
SOHO New Town
88 Jianguo Road
Chaoyang District
Beijing 100022
Tel: 86 10 6567 3333

Fax: 86 10 6568 6268
www.commune.com.cn

The Pink Loft
6 Sanlitun South Street
Chaoyang District
Beijing 100028
Tel: 8610 6506 8811

Simply Life
1d 5 Xintiandi
123 Xing Ye Road
Shanghai 200021
Tel: 86 21 6387 5100
enquiry@simplylife-sh.com
www.simplylife-sh.com

The Glamour Room
7/F, 5 The Bund
Shanghai 200002
Tel: 86 21 6350 9988
Fax: 86 21 6322 0099
info@m-onthebund.com
www.m-onthebund.com

TMSK
2 Xintiandi North
181 Tai Cang Road
Shanghai 200021
Tel: 86 21 6326 2227
Fax: 86 21 6326 2237
www.tmsk.com.cn

Fuchun Resort
Fuyang Section
Hangfu Yanjiang Road
Hangzhou, Zhejiang
China 311401
Tel: 86 571 6346 2999
Fax: 86 571 6346 1761

T8 Restaurant, Bar and Club
8 Xintiandi North
181 Tai Cang Road
Shanghai 200021
Tel: 86 21 6355 8999
Fax: 86 21 6311 4999

Xavier
Xintiandi North
181 Tai Cang Road
Shanghai 200021
Tel: 86 21 6328 7111
Fax: 86 21 6328 7333

Shanghai Trio
Unit 5, Bldg 1 Xintiandi
181 Tai Cang Road
Shanghai 200021
Tel/Fax: 86 21 6466 6884
Shanghai_trio@hotmail.com

Wood + Zapata
Unit 302, Building 28
Xintiandi, 181 Tai Cang

Road, Shanghai 200021
Tel: 86 21 6336 5183
Fax: 86 21 6336 5182
info@wood-zapata.com
www.wood-zapata.com

Kenneth Grant Jenkins
JK arQ, 14/F Times Square
Office Tower
93 Huai Hai Central Road
Shanghai 200021
Tel: 86 21 6391 0281
Fax: 86 21 5351 1589
ken-mego@online.sh.cn

The Hong Merchant
3, Lane 372
Xing Guo Road
Shanghai 200052
Tel: 86 21 6283 2696
Fax: 86 21 6283 9721
jpweber@uninet.com.cn

Simon Lee
Persimmon Home Store Ltd
Flat 3F, Ho Lee
Commercial Building
38-44 D'Aguilar Street
Central, Hong Kong
Tel: 852 2573 6626
Fax: 852 2573 6382

homedesign@persimmon-
home.com
www.persimmonhome.com

Jooi Design
Room 201-203
International Artists Factory
Lane 210 #3, Taikang Road
Shanghai 200025
Tel: 86 21 6473 6193
Fax: 86 21 3406 0010
trine@jooi.com
www.jooi.com

Tiramisu
Room 418
International Artists Factory
Lane 210 #3, Taikang Road
Shanghai 200025
Tel: 86 21 6472 6963
kim@tiramisushanghai.com
www.tiramisushanghai.com

Postkard
Room 210
International Artists Factory
Lane 210 # 3, Taikang Road
Shanghai 200025
Tel: 86 21 6473 8092
Fax: 86 21 6445 9909
askus@mailmanchina.com
www.postkard.com